Tips for Emotionally Healthy Successful Students

Ida Byrd-Hill

Upheaval Media, LLC

© 2013 Ida Byrd-Hill   All rights reserved.

No part of this book may be reproduced in any form or by any electronic or mechanical means including information storage and retrieval systems — except in the case of brief quotations embodied in critical articles or reviews, or in the case of the exercises in this book solely for the personal use of the purchaser – without permission in writing from the publisher, Upheaval Media, Inc.

Published by **Upheaval Media, LLC**.
P.O. Box 241488 Detroit, MI 48224

For **Group Book Orders and Speaking Engagements**
Call 877-429-2370   FAX 313-556-1669
info@upheavalmedia.net

Ida Byrd-Hill
K.I.S.S. Begins at Home
ISBN 978-0-9829610-2-5

Library of Congress Control Number: 2013936627

Dedication

I dedicate this book to my mother, Mary Byrd Williams, my father, William C. Byrd, and the teachers who groomed them as parents.

I owe my matriculation to the University of Michigan – Ann Arbor and my family's future legacy to my mother, a high school dropout, who initiated my lifelong learning process by visiting the school often, overseeing homework and educational activities at home. I still love reading, board games, puzzles, cultural institutions and traveling because of her parenting.

I owe my insatiable work ethic and entrepreneurial quest to my father, a high school dropout as well, who operated a trucking firm. He taught me to organize my talents into a business at a young age. I began my entrepreneur quest as a babysitter (***I am great with children.***), a baker (***I make delightful sweet treats.***), and newspaper deliver (***I developed a knack for finances.***).   Little did my father know I would develop talent for speaking as I was introverted my entire 17 years at home. (***I am a closet nerd.***)

Lastly, I thank the teachers who groomed my young parents. They were 18 and 19 when I was born. Their mothers were not around to show them how to be good parents so my teachers did.

Table of Contents

Why I Wrote This Book	5
Why You Need to Read this Book?	9
How to Read this Book	12
A Loving Atmosphere	13
A Rock Foundation	21
A Positive Thought	30
A Listening Ear	40
A Structured Discipline	47
A Productive Education	63
A Work Ethic	75
A Fun Playful Adventure	84
Homework Journal	93
Index	162

Why I Wrote This Book

I wrote this book in 2007 after a wonderful school my nonprofit, Uplift, Inc., had piloted, Hustle & TECHknow Preparatory High School closed. I had promised myself I would not publish it until I opened the predecessor school, INVENTech Academy. What I did not realize is that I would become so disillusioned with the education of so many gifted students in America. The students are getting smarter, but yet their academic performance on standardized tests has gotten worse. Once America led the industrialized world in education and now we are scraping the bottom. I hardly considered myself an expert although I have great love for children especially my own children, Kevin and Karen Hill. I believe America's education problem can be fixed with parent intervention.

Upon my children's birth, I dedicated my life to prepare them to be my legacy to the world. Today they are completing their sophomore years at Rochester Institute of Technology and Western Michigan University. Both are honor students. Getting them to this point as a single mom was no hocus-pocus. I determined the goals for their life and the path they should take. During our journey, I made the most unusual decision to remove my children from an affluent private school and usher them into the world of public schools namely, Detroit Public Schools. I made this decision so they would be able to experience the diverse African American population that exists and to embrace opportunities that could improve their overall community. Everyone thought I was crazy!. I am not. Professor Stern, an International Economist at the University of Michigan felt I should move into public policy 25 years. I did not. Ironically, as I wondered out loud why schools are not performing well, this wonderment turned in to a journey that led me to tinker with the schools my children attended to make them better. This tinkering led me to these results:

Hanstein Elementary
President of Parent Group   2002-2004
MEAP (*Michigan Standardized Educational test*) scores rose to **78%** in Reading and **69.1%** in Math in 2002-2003 from **28.1%** in Reading and **39.1%** in Math 2001-2002

- Created vision and mission for Parent Group
- Merged Parent Group mission with Principal mission
- Established action plan
- Instituted Classroom Parent System
- Organized two team building sessions with parents and teachers
- Convinced Parents to commit to 2 hours of extra homework daily
- Teachers agreed upon acceleration of the curriculum.
- Infused Family Fun Nights Academic oriented fun events
- Implemented Uniform Policy
- Established school store selling uniform tops

Duke Ellington Conservatory of Music and Art
Corresponding Secretary of Parent Group 2005-2006

- Orchestrated merger of two existing schools.
- Coordinated year long media blitz
- Increased Middle school MEAP scores from **44%** in Reading to **84%**
- Increased food service application collection from **44%** to **84%**
- Created parent newsletter The Drama distributed monthly

Created school blog
www.dukeellingtondrama.blogspot.com

Can you believe double-digit increases in standardized test scores twice????

There were many lessons learned over those 4 years, but nothing like the lessons I would learn when I secured a contract to operate an alternative high school for dropouts. I always wanted to build a boarding school for inner city students. Here was my chance. Unlike a boarding school that attracts the social elite, my school would be a school for dropouts and juvenile delinquents.

September 2006, Hustle & TECHknow was born. Yes, you did read, Hustle & TECHknow. Half the battle with attracting dropouts is attracting dropouts to a program that suits their needs. According to Claire Raines, author of *Connecting Generations: the Sourcebook*, Millennials, those ages 13 to 23 years of age, learning preferences are teamwork, technology, structure, entertainment and experiential activities. These students are considered technical natives having been raised with cell phones, DVDs, and video game consoles since their birth. They are naturally technical savvy.

This population loves the excitement and thrill of video games. Millennials can be found manipulating video games every day of the week for hours developing a skill of self-challenge. Major game retailers, such as EB Games and GameStop, have followed these Millennials, even to locations within the inner city.

They even joined in informal clubs to compete. They read complicated gaming magazines to decipher how to cheat the game and game systems. Their curiosity, intensity and seriousness about their video games are refreshing. I created this technology preparatory school with the entire curriculum online to simulate the video game action.

However, the irony of this story is that I secured a software corporation, Compuware Corporation as a partner. This technological powerhouse was the most perfect fit. It has global presence with 90 offices worldwide and a benevolent dictator, Peter Karmanos, who understands what it feels like to be a juvenile delinquent as he is a reformed one.

He had the fortune to meet a police officer who believed in his intelligence to fight for his entrance into the famed college preparatory high school, Cass Technical, where famous alumni such as Jerry Bruckheimer of Crime Scene Investigations were groomed.

The rest is history!!!! Peter Karmanos created Compuware Corporation, a 1.5 billion dollar software developer and relocated it into the heart of Downtown Detroit. Hustle & TECHknow is located there as well. Compuware employs 7500 of the nicest employees you have ever met.

My lofty goal is to transform these students into productive high performing professionals, like Peter Karmanos. Well, if the first year is any indication of the future we are well on our way. Here is synopsis of our first year:

- 80% Graduation Rate
- Collective Lexile Reading Grade Level Increased 4.2 to 7.8
- Business Protocol/Leadership Development Class completed by all students
- Satisfactory completion of Algebra I, Geometry or Trigonometry
- Entry into Oracle Thinkquest website design contest. *(Three teams)*
- Explorations & Exposures program launched
- Four Computer labs equipped with a computer for each student
- Establishment of Fencing team
- Implementation of School Dress uniform

> Winner of the Automation Alley Educational Program of the Year 2007

Little did I know that as I would teach them they would teach me the greatest lessons a parent can learn about reclaiming the lives of children, before, during and after childhood.

The main lesson I learned is that we, **PARENTS**, are our children's first teacher and we must reclaim our role to successfully educate our children, not at the schoolhouse but at home. Successful high performing schools are a collection of successful emotionally healthy kids. Successful emotionally healthy kids come from successful emotionally healthy homes. Our homes should power their hope for success. If we realign our values, beliefs and attitudes then we would produce successful emotionally healthy kids and hence successful emotionally healthy globally competitive schools. This book chronicles the lessons and wisdom I have learned. I hope this insight will put you onto the path of enlightenment into the craziest but most innovative period in your child's life. Enjoy K.I.S.S. Begins At Home

Why You Need to Read this Book?

Society is concerned about the education of today's children as our current and future standard of living is dependent upon the ability of young people to grow our corporations and industries. The No Child Left Behind Law looked at school performance collectively and attempted to manage school academic performance. It showed we are not globally competitive. Our industries need employees with creativity, imagination, critical thinking and risk taking. While these are admired qualities for our children, research shows children are becoming reckless risk takers at the age of 12.

Children of today are worried they have a bleak future. A liberal arts college degree once guaranteed them a job. Today it does not. Children need to focus on iSTEAM (invention, science, technology, engineering, arts and mathematics). Often, these are subjects they hate during their k-12 school years. They give up long before their life begins by becoming a risk taker. This risk taking leads them to make decisions negligent of consequences, including dropping out of school, never pursuing post-secondary training opportunities and gravitating toward crime.

Our job is to eliminate their fears and prepare them for the creative, technologically grounded future. Our job is to encourage them to have hope for the future and to instill into them a lifelong love for learning ever subject. When fail in our job to teach them to love learning, we see reckless, dangerous future zapping behavior.

Take the **Behavior Quiz** below to see if your child is too much of a risk taker. Check the statements that apply to your child.

BEHAVIOR QUIZ

- ☐ Are you visiting teachers often due to your child's behavior?
- ☐ Has your child experienced a drop in academic performance?
- ☐ Does your child struggle with basic family rules and expectations?
- ☐ Has your child ever been suspended, expelled from school?
- ☐ Is your child verbally abusive?
- ☐ Does your child associate with a bad peer group?
- ☐ Has your child lost interest in former activities, hobbies or sports?
- ☐ Do you have difficulty getting your child to do simple household chores?

- ☐ Has your child had problems with the law?
- ☐ Do you find yourself picking your words carefully when speaking to your child to avoid a verbal attack?
- ☐ Are you worried that your child may not finish high school?
- ☐ Does your child seem depressed/withdrawn?
- ☐ Has your child's appearance and/ or personal hygiene changed?
- ☐ Does your child ever display violent behavior?
- ☐ Is your child manipulative and/or deceitful?
- ☐ Does your child seem to demonstrate a lack of motivation?
- ☐ Do you suspect that your child sometimes lies or is dishonest with you?
- ☐ Are you concerned that your child may be sexually promiscuous?
- ☐ Has your child ever displayed any evidence of suicide ideation?
- ☐ Do you suspect at times that you have had other valuables stolen from your home?
- ☐ Does your child's behavior concern for your safety?
- ☐ Is your child angry or display temper outbursts?
- ☐ Does your child seem to lack self-esteem and self-worth?
- ☐ Do you have a lack of trust with your child?
- ☐ Does your child have problems with authority?
- ☐ Does your child engage in activities you do not approve of?
- ☐ Do you think your child is possibly using or experimenting with drugs/alcohol?
- ☐ Are you concerned about your child's well-being and their future?
- ☐ Does your child seem to constantly be in opposition to your family values?
- ☐ No matter what rules and consequences are established, does your child defy them?
- ☐ Are you exhausted and worn out from your child's defiant and/or destructive behavior and choices?

- ☐ When dealing with your child, do you often feel that you are powerless?
- ☐ Is your child on probation?

If you answered **yes** to seven or more of the above questions, your child is headed for trouble. Read K.I.S.S. Begins At Home to determine intervention strategies.

If you answered **yes** to eleven or more of the above questions, your child is in trouble K.I.S.S. Begins At Home to determine rescue strategies.

How to read this book

Read   Quote

Read   Passage

Flip to Homework Journal in the appendix. Match passage quotation to homework.

Complete homework

This book is organized with a quote summing up the passage followed by description of homework. Homework sheets are found in the appendix Homework Journal. You can find them by matching the quotation above the passage with the same quotation in the homework journal.

A Loving Atmosphere

Love the answer to the problem of human existence.

> Erich Fromm 1900-1980
> The Art of Loving 2.1 (1956)

Humans have an intense craving to be accepted by others, to be comforted by others, to belong. This craving is the impetus to be loved.

What is love? American Heritage Dictionary defines love as a deep, tender, ineffable feeling of affection and solicitude toward a person, such as that arising from kinship, recognition of attractive qualities, or a sense of underlying oneness The Bible in 1 Corinthians 13:4-8 states Love is patient; love is kind and envies no one. Love is never boastful, nor conceited, nor rude; never selfish, not quick to take offense. There is nothing love cannot face; there is no limit to its faith, its hope, and endurance. In a word, there are three things that last forever: faith, hope, and love; but the greatest of them all is love.

"Love is a sanctuary for our spirits, a bath of empathy for our emotions, a tranquil meadow in which to nurture our fond hopes and dreams." When love is present, the soul is at peace. Chaos and negativity fade away. Kindness and giving become commonplace. Joy and happiness, beyond current circumstances, radiates due to love. Everything becomes better when love touches.

At Hustle & TECHknow Preparatory High School, Virgil* came to school grumpy every day. One day I looked him in the eye and stated, "I love you!!!!" He stopped dead in his tracks and asked, "Do you really? He once walked slumped over; he now walks regal like a king. His grades and performance are college quality. In the past, they were poor, as he missed so many days in school.

Virgil is a survivalist. He has raised himself since he was 12 finding shelter and food wherever he can, as his mother is an alcoholic. He has chosen to remove himself from that environment. He comes to us every day knowing if no one else loves him, we at Hustle & TECHknow Preparatory High School love him. Today, I walk into every classroom every day and tell every student "I love you!!!!'

Collectively their grade point averages were .738 E - averages and now they are 2.13 C - averages.

COMPLETE #1 IN HOMEWORK JOURNAL

There is only one thing that has power and that is love.

> Alan Paton 1903-1988
> Cry the Beloved Country
> (1948)

Childhood is the craziest time in our life as we the parent realize we do not have any control over our children. We may send them to boot camps, boarding schools, boys and girls homes; juvenile detention facilities, therapy and sometimes we resort to whippings and beatings to adjust their behavior. Unfortunately, none of these will have a permanent effect upon a child unless love is present.

While children seem to abhor rules and discipline, they fully understand the bearer of rules have set these boundaries because they love them and want to ensure they will not be harmed in any way.

At Hustle & TECHknow Preparatory High School, if a student is caught smoking illegal substances then they are suspended for 10 school days. Jerome and Chris were caught smoking marijuana on the corner close to the school and were suspended for 10 school days. Jeremiah was so hurt that he disappointed the staff; he decided to plow himself into his English class that is accessible online. He completed 42 assignments during his timeout. (James at age 18 had dropped out of school in the eighth grade and this was his first attempt at high school.)

His rational: He knows we love him and he did not want to lose our love. When I asked him why he knew that, he replied, *"You always greet me with a smile and kind words."*

Smiles are contagious. Whenever a person smiles at you, it forces you to smile back. Often it appears we smile in return to be polite. However, the truth is that researchers discovered a theory entitled the "facial feedback" hypothesis. This hypothesis states that "involuntary facial movements provide sufficient peripheral information to drive emotional experience" Smiling changes your mood, your expression, and the world even if for a moment.

By the way, James came to school every day thereafter and he got into no more trouble. As a reward to his strong work ethic, he is employed by the Property Management of the building to clean our school.

COMPLETE #2 IN HOMEWORK JOURNAL

Human Nature is so constructed that it gives affection most readily to those who seem least to demand it.

> Bertrand Russell(1872-1970)
> The Conquest of Happiness
> 12, 1930

In the first week of Hustle & TECHknow Preparatory High School, we had a fight between Reggie and Aaron, who are best friends. As I debriefed Aaron, another teacher debriefed Reggie. She asked, *"Why are you fighting your best friend?"* He stated he was angry and he was tired of people dumping on him. She reached out to hug him and he cried in her arms like a baby. He later apologized for crying like that at age 18 but no one had hugged him since he turned seven.

Hugging is an intimate form of touch. We need to recognize that every human being has a profound physical and emotional need for touch – men, women and children.

We are alone in our separate bodies, yet to live we must connect with each other. Touch is the primary way we contact and connect with each other. Touch is the experience of how we meet each other. With touch, we meet the world outside of ourselves in a vibrant, alive, nourishing way. With touch, we meet, connect, bond, and belong. "Touching communicates. Touching heals," states Greg Godek, author of **Love, The Course They Forgot to Teach you in School** Without it, the only interaction people have is fights.

Dr. James Prescott, a neuropsychologist, and health scientist administrator at the National Institute of Health and Human Development in Bethesda, Maryland, researched 49 cultures and documented a strong relationship between less physical affection toward children and later aggression/violence.

In their first cross-cultural study, preschoolers in America were touched less and were more aggressive than preschoolers in France (Field, 1999). In that study, 40 French and American preschool children were observed on playgrounds with their parents and peers. The American parents watched and touched their children less than did the French parents. The American children played with, talked with, and touched their parents less and were more aggressive toward their parents. During peer interactions, the American children touched their peers less, grabbed their peers' toys more, showed more aggression toward their peers, and showed more fussing.

In a study, adolescents' intimacy with parents and friends was noted to be a protective factor (Field et al., 1995). Students who had greater intimacy (a hug) with their parents had greater interest in school, higher self-esteem, lower depression, and lower risk-taking scores.

Hugs have the power to make someone feel cherished.... the power to give *(and receive at the very same time!)* kindness, warmth, tenderness, support, healing, security - and most of all belonging. All with a simple touch - a simple hug.

Feeling strongly about this research and seeing the benefits of hugs have upon children, I gave Hustle & TECHknow Preparatory High School teachers the license to hug, especially the boys as many of them received little or no hugs as parents feel this interaction is feminine. The students' wild violent behavior calmed down dramatically in a short amount of time.

COMPLETE #3 IN HOMEWORK JOURNAL

Show Kindness to your Parents.

> Muhammad (A.D. 570-632)
> Quran 6.151

At Hustle & TECHknow Preparatory High School, we realized our students and their families were so battered by the struggles of life that in order to transform the students we needed to transform the family. We created an event *The Touch of Love* to continue the hug fest to our families.

Our program thanked parents for trusting our school to groom their student. We, the staff and students, distributed flowers to the parents. Since everyone is not comfortable with physical kisses, we distributed mini organza favor bags of Hershey chocolate kisses to say "**I love you!!!!**" followed by a light candlelit dinner decorated with romantic red tablecloths and all.

The next day students randomly stopped by my office to pick up some kisses. Students calmed even more.

COMPLETE #4 IN HOMEWORK JOURNAL

A

Rock

Foundation

A home is not a mere transient shelter; its essence lies in its permanence's, in its capacity for accretion and solidification.

> H. L. Mencken (1880---1924)
> "On Living in Baltimore"
> Prejudices: Faith Series 1924

Today's, people are moving from house to house in an effort or worst yet to avoid paying rent beyond the security deposit. Worse yet, increase their investment potential in a house.

Either way, students are suffering from the instability caused by this movement. My friends have had friends for life; friends who saw them through acne, buck teeth, and pig tails. These friends know all of their comical stories as they grew up together from birth. They have comfort in knowing they had a network of friends nearby. Today, students are missing a stable network of family or friends nearby. Sadly, many do not even know their neighbors who live right next door, let alone down the street. They have not lived in their neighborhood long enough to develop those relationships.

Back in the day, network of neighbors and friends saved many children from their foolish decisions and mistakes. The world is changing so rapidly around us. Global competition requires students to embrace and manipulate change.

Stability gives students the foundation to deal with the changes that are happening so rapidly in our world today. This stability is akin to the roots of an oak tree. When it is little, it is easy to pluck the roots, and replant the tree. If you replant a tree, too often, the tree will die. However if the tree is left there for years it will develop deep roots, a strong trunk and large branches. The older oak tree can withstand tornadoes hurricanes while the younger would break or snap with any strong wind. Students are the same. If given the opportunity to develop strong roots, they too will grow stronger.

Many of the students at Hustle & TECHknow Preparatory High School have spent a chunk of their child hood homeless. They are fragile like a little oak tree as they have no roots. Amazingly, their extended families and friends have come to their rescue when they discovered the commitment they have to our school.

Let your students develop into a strong oak tree.

COMPLETE #5 IN HOMEWORK JOURNAL

I've never been poor only broke. Being poor is a frame of mind. Being broke is only a temporary situation.

> Mike Todd (1909—1958)
> Death of a Showman,
> Newsweek 31 March 1958

Often, we use the term 'poor' and 'broke' interchangeably. Yet, they are not the same. Being broke is a temporary state. A person, who spends all the cash they have in their wallet, is broke. A cash infusion can remedy being broke. However, cash cannot remedy poverty; for poverty is a state of mind. Poverty is generated from the thought of lack and scarcity. People fear not having enough. This thought of lack becomes a self-fulfilling prophecy.

A poor person cannot see opportunities around them, or they expect opportunities to be laid at their feet rather than work for them. A poor person sees the negative even in the positive. Within the United States, opportunities and jobs are plenteous, business contracts are growing, yet some people are walking around in pity complaining that opportunities are not available. Poverty is a state of mind that prevents one from forward growth in career, life, expectations etc.

A poor person lives for instant gratification. Their money is spent on items to ease the pain of existing each day as they feel they will not have enough to last tomorrow. If you give a poor person a million dollars today, one year in the future they will not have any money left to live on. Our greatest entertainers and athletes earn millions only to die or retire broke. Why? They have never been cured from the disease of poverty. Nevertheless, they are not the only people suffering from this disease. People from all walks of life – factory workers, doctors, lawyers even business people are plagued with this disease. This disease impairs a person's ability to create and accumulate assets. Assets accumulation requires goal setting, vision—the ability to see positive rising from negative, initiative, responsibility, characteristics the poor usually lack.

If you are poor or suffer from the disease of poverty, don't despair, there is a cure. The cure is simple. Change your thoughts to abundance. The human mind merely grows what we plant. Plant thoughts of abundance and you automatically see opportunities you never saw before. You then get the courage to seize, manipulate and grow these opportunities. These opportunities turn into cash. This cash flow can be accumulated into investments, hence you are now rich.

Changing your thoughts to abundance is difficult, as it requires you to reprogram your mind. It requires the discipline of immediately replacing a negative thought with a positive thought the minute the negative thought occurs. It requires the shedding of old habits for new habits. It requires the removal of negative people until you can learn to deal with them.

Are You Poor?

1. Are your friends' constant complainers?
2. Do you complain about the lack of opportunity?
3. Do you lack goals with forward direction?
4. Do you live from paycheck to paycheck?
5. Do you have any savings or investments?
6. Do you constantly worry about your finances?
7. Do you pamper physical items, such as furniture as if you will never get any other items?
8. Do you shop for luxuries before paying your bills?
9. Do you spend the bulk of your money on consumable items, such as clothes?
10. Is your car payment greater than your house payment?

If you answered **yes** to two or more of these questions, **YOU ARE POOR**!

Most of our struggles at Hustle & TECHknow Preparatory High School is that most students and their parents are stricken with the disease of poverty. So stricken they have forgotten how to dream and see any positivity.

Disclaimer: Positive thoughts do not stop negative things from occurring in your life. Life is 10% of what actually happens to you and 90% of how you respond to what happens to you. Positive thought determines our response to be creative giving us the ability to rebound from the negativity.

COMPLETE #6 IN HOMEWORK JOURNAL

A man is rich whose income is larger than his expenses and he is poor if his expenses are greater than his income.

> La Bruyere (1645 – 1696)
> "Of Gifts of Fortune" (49)
> The Characters 1688

Have you ever dreamed of driving a Bentley, Rolls Royce or Mercedes or living in a palatial mansion in Beverly Hills, CA, Palm Beach, FL, Scottsdale, AZ, Grosse Pointe, MI, White Plains, NY, Buckhead, GA? Alternatively, have ever you dreamed of wearing a Rolex watch? Have you ever dreamed of eating caviar, stuffed artichokes or lobster every day of the week? Better yet, you have dreamed of being pampered by a butler, nanny, maid and a cook? Think again. There are some Millionaires who live this lifestyle. However, the mass majority of them do not.

Millionaires' traits usual go counter to the perceptions the public has of Millionaires. For Example:

Perception: Millionaires spend lots of money on high-end luxury items.
Reality: Millionaires are tightwads, living well below their means.

Millionaires love quality items at discounted prices. They buy $350 suits rather than $1,500 Hugo Boss suit or they buy Hugo Boss suits on sale. They do wear Timex watches rather than Rolex watches. They drive American cars rather than luxury foreign cars. They shop at high-end department stores but usually find a deal. Ironically, you can find them at the discount warehouse stores located in ritzy areas like Costco or Sam's Club.

Perception: Millionaires are frivolous spenders.
Reality: Millionaires are meticulous budgeters and investors.

Most Millionaires plan their spending finding places to save money to accumulate cash to get what they desire. They know where every penny has been spent. I realized, in my children's 10th grade year, I would not have enough money to prepare for their graduation and college search. I refused to purchase another car and rode the bus. The car note, insurance, maintenance and gas cost $1200 per month. The monthly bus pass for me and my children was $210 per month. I took half the savings and moved to a larger house in a better neighborhood. My children hated the change. But they are successfully entrenched in college today.

Millionaires meticulous disposition is not just related to budgeting, Millionaires are detailed investors. Fifty percent of their wealth is in publicly traded stocks/mutual funds and pension plans. They usually prescribe the "Buy and Hold" method of investing. The rest of their wealth is in their private business and real estate.

In fact, many may not even know who millionaires may be. I was sitting at dinner with a client who just crossed the $5.8 million-dollar net worth mark. At the end of dinner, the waitress handed me the bill, as I looked more affluent. The client and I chuckled, as people have no clue he is worth $5.8 million net. Millionaires walk amongst us all day. They many even live next door.

If you really want to be a millionaire, invest in reading the book "**The Millionaire Next Door**" by Thomas Stanley and keeping a monthly budget.

COMPLETE #7 IN HOMEWORK JOURNAL

When you are poor, you grow up fast.

> Billie Holiday (1915 -1959)
> Lady Sings the Blues, 1956

Children are losing their innocence by twelve. The youthful, playful innocence of children – also known as foolishness, has been replaced with street wisdom as children are raising themselves. They are burdened with finding their own shelter, providing their own food and clothes; things parents should do.

Worse yet, parents provide these things but spend little time playing or talking to their children, leaving them emotionally poor responsible for creating emotional instability. Physically and mentally, children are poorly equipped to raise themselves. They need the wisdom and stability of adults to instill in them the character and values necessary to thrive in today's' society. Child hood should be the best carefree, portion of a person's life. Our children are being robbed of their youth. This thievery comes with a price – aggressive, angry, ill prepared, and non-educated youth.

This society can no longer afford this price. We must fight against stripping our youth of their innocence causing them to springing up without the necessary grooming. We must re-instill their innocence. We must give them their hood back. Despite their juvenile records and their size, Hustle & TECHknow Preparatory High School students are children. We have injected childish activities within the school day to revive their innocence even if it is for 6 hours a day.

COMPLETE #8 IN HOMEWORK JOURNAL

A

Positive

Thought

Man is not the creature of circumstance, circumstance are the creatures of men. We are free agents, and man is more powerful than matter.

> Benjamin Disraeli (1804—1881)
> Vivian Grey 6,7 1826

My belief has always been that I would become wealthy even while I lived in a HUD housing project in Flint, MI. Despite the extreme cockroaches, crime, and seedy landscape, I believed I would be wealthy. Every action followed that belief. When other tenants tolerated the high grass, I cut it with the used lawnmower I purchased. I planted a colorful flower garden. This belief was also reflected in my job choices. In high school, when everyone worked a minimum wage job at the local fast food restaurant, I worked at the library as a page. I loved and still love to read. My passion for books allowed me to earn 1 ½ times minimum wage. My grades were excellent affording a college scholarship to the University of Michigan. While the scholarship only paid for tuition and room and board, I was forced to work to achieve my goal – cash upon graduation. Every job I received earned at least 2 times minimum wage. My belief was that I deserved better than average and that is what I got. Rich thoughts drew me to rich experienced jobs. Opportunities after college seemed to abound as I only saw opportunity.

However, as easily as opportunities came, they went. I married a man who believed in scarcity. No matter what opportunities were available, he saw lack, scarcity, and poverty. Despite our six-figure family income, we struggled for nine years because the thoughts of scarcity and poverty were dominant.

When I divorced him and negative thoughts left, my opportunities began to rebound. WHY? The universe contains both abundance and scarcity, rich and poor, good and bad! Whatever we think upon is attracted to us.

Your circumstances manifest your thoughts. Hustle & TECHknow Preparatory High School and my house looks the way I feel -- modern and wealthy. No matter how much money I have, if I felt poor my surrounding would look poor. Despite the fact, students enter a modern luxurious school, we struggle with graffiti and nastiness as students believe they only deserve nastiness. We are making a slow impact in changing their thoughts hoping we can rescue them from the 'hood.'

COMPLETE #9 IN HOMEWORK JOURNAL

Everything you can imagine is real

Pablo Picasso (1881- 1973)

Wayne Dyer in his book "You'll see it when you believe it" sums it up in this manner. "Whatever you focus your thoughts on expands!" If you have a scarcity mentality, it means that we believe in scarcity and that we evaluate our life in terms of its lack. If we dwell on scarcity, we are putting energy into what we do not have and this continues to be our experience of life. When you live and breathe prosperity with a belief that everything is in huge supply and that we are all entitled to have all that we can. You start actively treating yourself and others in this fashion.

Prosperity and abundance is not something that you can manufacture but something that you accept or tune into. Unlimited prosperity and abundance is all around us. The issue is, Can You See It? The answer is, Only If You Believe It! Belief can be summed up by this poem.

> If you *think* you are beaten, you are
> If you *think* you dare not, you don't
> If you like to win, but you *think* you can't
> It is almost certain you won't.
>
> If you *think* you'll lose, you're lost
> For out in the world we find
> Success begins with a fellow's will
> It's all in the *state of mind*.
>
> If you *think* you are outclassed, you are,
> You've got to *think* high to rise
>
> You've got to be *sure of yourself* before
> You can ever win a prize
>
> Life's battles don't always go

> To the stronger or faster man,
> But soon or late the man who wins
> Is the man **WHO THINKS HE CAN**

At Hustle & TECHknow Preparatory High School, we scheduled a Social Responsibility class to indoctrinate students on time management, planning and positive thinking. They initially fought the idea of the class until we began our field trip program, Explorations & Exposures that allowed them to experience other nice environments.

COMPLETE #10 IN HOMEWORK JOURNAL

Death and life are in the power of the tongue.

> Proverbs 18:21
> The Bible (King James Version)

The tongue is capable of giving an individual life or killing a person. Have you ever had someone tell a lie about you. Did you feel like you could die on the inside? How do you feel when someone gives you a compliment? I feel so alive. Words are powerful. In the past century it was said "sticks and stones make break my bones but words will never hurt me." That adage is not true. Words have the ability to stab someone in the chest and carve out their heart; heal the pain as if it never occurred.

Many juvenile delinquents have repeatedly heard negative sayings *"you can't do anything right!" "You are ugly," "You are stupid" "You will never amount to anything."* No matter how intelligent they are, every time they are faced with a decision, great or small, their subconscious mind replays those *sayings*, causing them to procrastinate in making the decision, hence fulfilling the prophecy *"you can't do anything right!"* These old mental tapes, positively or negatively, create our lives.

Therefore, when the math facilitator/ coach was having difficulty in motivating the students to complete their math assignments online, I decided to camp out in his classes as Facilitator for 1 week. The first day I told all four classes, **"you are math wizards as I have seen you count money.** *I don't care what other teachers have told you. Math is easy."* I gave them their homework assignments they did not complete those assignments.

The second day I told them, **"Math has nothing to do with numbers. Math is about the relationship numbers have with each other. If you memorize the rules regarding the relationship math is easy. You all are smart enough to memorize the rules."** I gave them homework math rules to write down, they did half of it.

The third day I told them, ***"Wizards are masters of their craft. If you are a math wizard then you must master math. The only way you can do that is by completing the homework which by the way is math vocabulary."*** They completed all the homework from that point on which is usually math rules and vocabulary. Needless to say, all four classes lived up to my words that they are math wizards. They completed their classes on schedule even though we were behind schedule. I even had two students complete Algebra 4/ Trigonometry in 45 days flat.

The most interesting development is the giggles and excitement that exuded during math class. One of the other coaches assumed there was no coach in the room and stepped into tell the students to be quiet. I laughed. I was most touched when Ashley checked out a Mastering Algebra book from the library. Her book discussed the language of math, which I promptly copied and assigned as homework. She told me a few of my students met at the library after school, but they did not want me to know.

Today a few of those students want to be engineers, car designers and architects as we discovered their love for math especially Davison, who has wanted to be an electrical engineer for a long time but gave up on his dream when he struggled with basic math.

Although I knew the tongue could be a self-fulfilling prophecy, nothing convinced me of this fact more than these classes. Parent, you have the power to speak your children to become an executive, president whatever no matter what environment you live in. You have the power to make them SOB's. You decide what you speak. Don't let their behavior decide what you speak. Speak them into a higher station in life. Even if they don't arrive at the exact station, they will be much higher than their current station in life.

COMPLETE #11 IN HOMEWORK JOURNAL

Self-control and self-esteem vary directly. The more self-esteem a person has, the greater, as a rule, is his desire, and his ability to control himself.

> Thomas S. Szasz (1920 --)
> Control and Self Control
> Heresies, 1976

Sad to say, most people in the world have no self-esteem in their abilities. Those who publicly brag about their accomplishments have no self-esteem in their abilities. The greedy philosophy of the 1980's—keeping up with the Jones'—was built upon people's perception of how others viewed their worth. People easily succumb to criticism (both positive and negative) of colleagues and relatives. Many refuse to take risk, even calculated risk, in their lives and careers as they fear criticism from others saying, ("*That's a crazy idea! Oh that won't work!*") and deeper yet, criticism from themselves. How many times have you said to yourself, "I can't do that because..." the fear of criticism is related to one's self esteem. The lower the self-esteem, the greater the fear of criticism. The greater the self-esteem, the lower the fear of criticism.

Many children have low self-esteem and so do many parents. How you see your self determines your actions and conversation. As parents, especially single moms, we see ourselves as victims as society keeps telling us we are. We are moms. What they don't tell is moms, single or marriage are doing the job of two parents.

Students make dumb decisions in an attempt to belong with their peers. We utilized peer pressure to create an environment of productivity. Students are assigned to classes based on their math performance. Students are excluded from field trips and programs based on non-performance. Since students want to belong so they step up their performance.
COMPLETE #12 IN HOMEWORK JOURNAL

Success is the ability to go from one failure to another with no loss of enthusiasm.

> Sir Winston Churchill
> (1874—1965)

Successful people know their lives are riddled with failure. "Failure is only a temporary defeat—nature's way of readjusting your plan." Accept it as so. Many ordinary people have accepted failure and then gone on to greatest.

Thomas Edison *"failed"* 10,000 times before he perfected the modern light bulb. His assistant frustrated by the many attempts questioned Edison about their dilemma. Edison response was "Yes, we have experimented with this thing 8,999 times, but I know there are 8,999 materials that won't work' and forged ahead. Edison had no formal education to remind him that he had failed. All he had was a dream that a fireless candle could be invented.

"Every adversity, every failure, every headache carries with it, the seed of an equivalent or greater benefit. When adversities, failures or headaches occur, success equal to or greater than those failures will come.

Are there patterns and habits that keep repeating themselves? Unfortunately, we never realize what the patterns and habits are so we keep repeating them until failure occurs.

Failure to a child is life ending. They will choose not to participate in something –what if I fail? Their lives are riddled with failure and yet they survive. In the 'hood' the reverse is true; will my family still love me if I become somebody? Children are fearful of success.

Our mantra is this poem written by Marianne Williams in **Return to Love**

Our deepest fear is not that we are inadequate.
Our deepest fear is that we are powerful beyond measure.
It is our light, not our darkness that frightens us.
We ask ourselves, who am I to be brilliant, gorgeous, talented and fabulous?
Actually, who are we not to be?
You are a Child of God.
Your playing small doesn't serve the world.
There's nothing enlightened about shrinking so that other people won't feel insecure around you.
We were born to make manifest the glory of God that is within us.
It's not just in some of us, it's in everyone.
And as we let our light shine, we unconsciously
Give people permission to do the same.
As we are liberated from our own fears,
Our presence automatically liberates others.

As an entrepreneur I have suffered more failure than one can admit. Nonetheless, I dust myself off reflect on why I started the project, what lessons did the failure teach and begin again.

Learn the lesson in the failure and begin again. Let your children, FAIL. Failure is the best lesson. We are always attempting to save them from failure. If failure is life threatening we should. If it is not, we should not. Our best gift is to give them room to fail and advice to begin again.

COMPLETE #13 IN HOMEWORK JOURNAL

A

Listening

Ear

Nothing has a stronger influence psychologically on their environment and especially on their children than the unlived life of the parent

Carl Jung (1881- 1973)

The American Dream, is to be a happily married couple living in 2000 to 3500 square foot home in an affluent neighborhood decorated by a professional interior designer, wearing the latest fashions purchased at Bloomingdale's, Saks Fifth Avenue, Macys, Parisian or Neiman's. Your children would attend a prestigious private or public schools. You would belong to the prominent country club, yacht club and/or social clubs. You would even vacation amongst the wealthy at exotic locations around the world. Everyone knows and respect you. So many young professionals want to be like you.

Here's reality: Alarm buzzes at 5:00 am. You slowly arise, stumbling to the gym for a workout. You then shower. Get dressed. Wakeup the children and get them dressed. Prepare breakfast to be eaten now or maybe in the car on the run. Drop the kids off at daycare or school. Jump on the highway for the grueling drive *(or should I say parking lot)* to work. Get to work and deal with demanding clients and get undermined politically by your boss. You want to scream yet you smile while containing your anger.

The clock chimes 5:00 pm work still not done. Back into the car, arrive at home, vegetated by the rush hour only to find You forgot to pickup kids from schools. Once home, you listen to your children's story. Cook dinner. Review their home work. Get them to bed. You retire to the bedroom exhausted only to prepare for another day to make another dollar. you realize you are really lonely although you are surrounded by children, spouse or significant other. You finally drift off to sleep by the hum of the TV.

Our lives continue to spiral these scenes over and over again. Before we know it years have whizzed by and we ask ourselves "what have we accomplished?"

We have accomplished "depression, stress and anxiety" as stated by 60 percent of the sample group of Douglas LaBier's book, **Modern Madness**. We have developed high blood pressure, heart attacks and strokes at earlier ages. Even though more and more Americans have reached the success level of money, power and position we have lost ourselves, our life of personal fulfillment and meaning. Although we are making more money than ever, our consumer debt has escalated to 984 billion or $3500 per , man or woman. **"Debt is one of our main shackles. Our levels of debt and our lack of savings make the nine to five routine mandatory. Between our mortgages, car financing and credit card debts, we cannot afford to quit any job"** even if it makes us sick. The very essence of our lives is sucked from us as we begrudgingly occupy a job/career/ lifestyle that now bores or depresses us. But what can we do?

Vicariously, we hold these trappings near and dear to our hearts. Society even praises us for acquiring these trappings. These social circles define our external lives. Do we attempt to maintain the American Dream even though it is killing us or our families. We are in a lifestyle funk as we are on a treadmill and cannot get off. We pat ourselves on the back that we are not living the life of common people. Your children, sensitive to the negative vibes of your funk, are reacting in manners not appropriate for affluent children. You acknowledge their craziness only to blame television, video games and schools for presenting so much violence. It isn't the television, video games or schools driving your children crazy, it is your lifestyle. You must do something different.

COMPLETE #14 IN HOMEWORK JOURNAL

Children have never been very good at listening to their elders, but they have never failed to imitate them.

James Baldwin (1881- 1973)

Living in the world of capitalism it is easy to fall into a lifestyle funk. We are not judged by our personalities alone; but rather we receive social status by the things we own, the jobs we hold, the income we generate, the cash we accumulate. This social status is determined by two things: cash accumulation or good credit. If you lose your good credit, you can use cash to restore it. Lose your cash and you will soon lose your good credit. With that loss, you will be relegated to second-class citizenry where you get poor services and poor treatment. Most people can lose things but the poor treatment warps their self-esteem. We would avoid it at all cost.

We pretend we are not in a lifestyle funk except our children are crazy. Their behavior leaves a lot to be desired. They should be mild mannered well-behaved young people on track to outperform you educationally, financially and emotionally, but they are not. Children imitate your behavior. If they are crazy then they are probably reacting to our vibes. If you are still not sure you are in a lifestyle funk, Take this Lifestyle Funk Quiz.

COMPLETE #15 IN HOMEWORK JOURNAL

When people talk, listen completely. Most people never listen.

                          Ernest Hemingway
                          (1899-1961)

Stephen Covey in **Living the 7 Habits** state" *Children want to talk to their parents. They want to open up; they want to feel it is safe."* I have found they want to talk on their time frame, which may not be your timeframe. One of our students, Chris, has been with us for 6 months but he had not bonded to any staff member primarily as he was angry with me. I had him served house arrest twice for violating his probation that required his attendance at school every day. One day he needs to see me now! He tells me he is in trouble Well that is the summary of the 1 ½-hour conversation he had. His frustration caused him to spill his entire guts. I ended the conversation with some advice. Three days later he stops by the office and state *"Miss Ida you were right."* He thanked me with a hug that brought tears to my eyes. In his eyes, I went from being the Devil to being an Angel. We had finally made a breakthrough with this student. When he stopped in I was so busy attempting to prepare a report for Detroit Public Schools, yet I took the time to talk to him. Those two hours changed his behavior and work performance forever.

When he went to court, yes, he was a juvenile delinquent, his social worker, probation officer and judge were amazed at his report card. His grade point average moved from a D average to a B average. I grinned from ear to ear like a proud Momma. My baby was finally making a transformation. I expect he will graduate from high school soon.

COMPLETE #16 IN HOMEWORK JOURNAL

The character of a man is known from his conversations.

                        Menander
                        (342 BC – 291 BC)

Listen to a person and you will discover the values that guide their lives. It doesn't take a lifetime it just takes 30 minutes. If they cheat and steal, they will tell you of their scandals. If they are a hard worker and the table needs the dishes removed, they will remove them without any one asking. If they bring you gossip, then they are a gossiper. If they are always talking about things, they are materialistic. If the subject of their conversation is always themselves, they are probably selfish. If they apply for federal assistance while employed at a job you know they are not honest.

Often, we fail to really listen to the verbal and non-verbal clues individuals provide us as we really do believe what they state does not apply to us. We really want to believe there is good in everyone and the negativity we see is not real.

Listen to what people say and don't say. Listen to their personality. Listen to their heart. Listen with you heart and you will never be fooled. People are exactly as you sum them up. Their spiritual vibe always tells the truth even if they do. Trust your heart and learn from it.

COMPLETE #17 IN HOMEWORK JOURNAL

A Structured Discipline

A Man's Character is his Fate.

> Heraclitus
> On the Universe
> 540 BC – 480BC

> Sow a thought, Reap an action
> Sow an action, reap a habit
> Sow a habit, reap a character
> Sow a character, reap a destiny

No matter what philosophy becomes popular, the fundamentals of success are these old fashion values:

> Humility
> Temperance
> Courage
> Justice
> Patience
> Industrious
> Simplicity
> Honesty

A simple enduring modest attitude guided by self-restraint, fairness, and truth fueled by hard work will allow an individual to arrive at the top of ladder of success. People have attempted to steal success by employing these newfound values:

> Arrogance
> Excessiveness
> Cowardice
> Suspicion
> Impatience
> Obscurity
> Intricate
> Deceitful

Old-fashioned values require a slow but steady process. In our fast-paced world, it appears that the process works. They do but only for a short time as the Universe is governed by the sowing reaping principle. Plant 1 kernel of corn and receive an entire stalk corn with thousands of kernels of corn. The same concept works in life.

Sow thievery--Reap massive thievery of life
Sow manipulation—Reap enormous manipulation

The issue isn't "if " the reaping occurs; it is "when." Reaping always occurs. Either embrace these values and generate a stellar reputation based on them, or repel these values and generate a non-reputable reputation based on the lack of them.

COMPLETE #18 IN HOMEWORK JOURNAL

The thing that impresses me the most about America is the way parents obey their children.

>King Edward VIII
>(1884 – 1972)

While we want to have a relationship with our children where they talk to us during their child years, we are not their friends or buddies. Most parents have an important profession to transform klutzy children into healthy self-confident productive adults. We have 18 years to instill good values and processes into our children. We are not here to give them everything they desire. We are not here to succumb to their commands, tantrums, or demands.

We must ensure our family is a collection of interwoven individuals who depend upon one another rather than a collection of individuals who live under the same roof. We must ensure our children have consistent chores as it teaches them responsibility and work ethic. We must get involved in their education to ensure they graduate high school and post-secondary options. We must teach them to respect authority, systems and institutions while we teach them to change the world. We must know the friends they select and hang out with. We must meet their friends' parents to understand the values they are teaching. We must return to family dinner so that we can talk to our children and get to know the values they live by.

We must reassume our throne as parents. For when we do, we will produce emotionally stable productive children who may hate our decisions today, but appreciate them later, as we assist them avert the dangers of childhood.

At Hustle & TECHknow Preparatory High School, I served as the General. I refused to accept students' excuses, their blatantly urbane behavior. I insisted on excellence, respect, and courtesy. Ironically, even if they did not give those items to others they always gave them to me. Students rise to expectations of the parent figures around them. So set expectations that cause them to live up to something.

COMPLETE #19 IN HOMEWORK JOURNAL

There is a measure in everything. There are fixed limits beyond which and short of which right cannot find a resting place.
                        Horace
                        Roman lyric poet & satirist
                        (65 BC - 8 BC)

Once children receive adult size bodies, parents gladly provide them the freedom of adults, going where they choose when they choose, with whom they choose. These young people get in all sorts of problem even infringing the law. Simple rules would prevent such occurrences. While children abhor rules, they understand they are a sign of a caring adult.

At Hustle & TECHknow Preparatory High School, I got extremely upset with Raymond, who was speaking on his cell phone during math class. I asked him for his cell phone which he failed to turn over. I proceeded to take the phone. Before we both knew it, we were standing nose to nose in an altercation stance. Eventually Raymond hopped over two cubicles and left.

Ironically, Raymond returned the next day on time. I had planned on suspending him for 3 days. Before executing judgment, I always have a conference with the student. I walked down Monroe with Raymond only to discover he was sleeping on the streets as his mother put him out of his house for disobeying her rules. According to Raymond that was a rouse as he had no rules. He was never at home before 11 pm and he went straight to bed. He was really upset no one cared enough about him to impose any rules. He knows he should have a curfew. He knows he should have a bedtime. I asked him, *"why did you return to school today?"* His response " Miss Ida I believe you care about me even though you discipline us as you always have time to listen to us." I look at Raymond with this puzzled look on my face. He explains further, *"rules state a parent cares enough about you to set boundaries to keep you safe."* I laugh *" I guess I really care about you then!!!!!"*

COMPLETE #20 IN HOMEWORK JOURNAL

Right discipline consists, not in external compulsion, but in habits of mind, which lead spontaneously to desirable rather than undesirable activities.

> Bertand Russell (1872-1970)
> On Education: Especially in Early Childhood 1, 1926

As I stood in the middle of Monroe hugging this handsome but troubled young man, I seethed with anger. Many of the troubles young people face would be eliminated with the establishment and execution of rules. Rules loudly scream care and concern. Rules provide stability and tradition. Here are a few simple rules every child should have:

Curfew is home by the time the sun is setting unless working a job or participating in a school sanctioned activity. One hour after closing time for either.

Homework completed prior to visiting friends or social events.

Homework is to be completed at home or library. This rule insures good grades as homework is the key to school success.

Ask permission for social itinerary prior to execution. This rules tells you their every move.

Call from your friends' home on a landline upon arrival there. These rules confirm their every move. The cell phone unless it has a GPS tracker does not.

Bedtime during the week is 8:00 pm ages 0 -8, 9pm ages 9-14 and 10:00 pm. 15-18 years old. This rule allows children to develop strong bodies as they need 8 – 10 hours of sleep as their bodies are still growing

Home for dinner by 6:00 or 7:00 pm. This rule enforces good nutrition as they get a home cooked meal. It also sets the stage for regular family discussions over the meal. People tend to talk more over food.

Children cannot visit friends' house until you have met their parents.

Family date night is never to be broken. This rule forces family together time regularly where children have their parents undivided attention from the cares of the world.

Can't verbalize the major rules in your house, then neither can your children. By the way, **" Becuase I said so is not a rule."** Give them some sure fire boundaries that you will never deviate from.

COMPLETE #21 IN HOMEWORK JOURNAL

Nothing is stronger than habits

> Ovid 43BC – 17AD
> Ars Amatoria

Habits are *re-current*, often-unconscious patterns of behavior that are acquired through frequent *repetition*. These behaviors and actions we perform without conscious thought. These actions are simple, such as brushing our teeth, the way we organize our houses, the way we dress. These habits define who we are and what we do. They define our character.

They can be good, such as arriving at meetings on time, saving 15% of your income; or they can be bad habits like smoking marijuana weekly. Nevertheless, they are the only things we change albeit with much struggle.

While psychologist state it takes 21 days to create a new habit; it actually takes more time and consistency to form a new habit. But, it can be done.

At Hustle & TECHknow Preparatory High School, children, albeit young in age, have formed bad habits such as rolling their eyes or shoplifting or smoking marijuana. Some habits they have chosen for themselves. Others they have learned at home from their parents.

Parents' habits unconsciously are transmitted to their children as children mimic our behaviors and actions. Change our actions and behaviors change their action and behaviors.

COMPLETE #22 IN HOMEWORK JOURNAL

A Goal Without a Plan is Just a Wish.

>Antoine de Saint – Exypery
>1900—1944

Goal setting has become the mantra of the last two decades. Every motivational speaker talks about writing down your goals. But, a goal without a plan is just a wish. To achieve a goal there must be an incremental daily plan to achieve those goals.

Every human being has secret desires, goals, and wishes. Unfortunately, only 3% write down their goals. That 3% controls the entire world as illustrated by the Forbes 400 list.

When someone writes down any goal, it becomes a part of the conscious and subconscious mind. The subconscious mind attempts to develop a plan execution, to achieve the goal. If an individual writes down the plan then it becomes a matter of completing each task.

Students at Hustle & TECHknow Preparatory High School complete a set of questionnaires to secure information to complete their educational development plan. This plan details their career, potential college programs and scholarship to pay for college. Ironically, students appear to be more focused on their studies as they have a sense of direction.

COMPLETE #23 IN HOMEWORK JOURNAL

He who every morning plans the transaction of the day and follow out that plan, carries a thread that will guide him through the maze of the most busy life. But where no plan is laid, where the disposal of time is surrendered merely to the chance of incidence, chaos will soon reign.

> Victor Hugo 1802—1885

Chaos is evidence of no planning. Where chaos abounds trouble comes. Trouble creates stress, depression and a sense of failure. If your life is full of trouble, take the time to write down your plans for each day the proceeding evening. Chaos in both your personal and professional lives will be reduced to a minimum.

Hustle & TECHknow Preparatory High School student's review their goals weekly. This plan assists them in focusing on their daily requirement to achieve their life's goals. Completion of these requirement leads to completion of their goals, which they write daily. They hate it! A new student Tamara states "Miss Ida I am finally making headway with my life. Planning does work."

COMPLETE #24 IN HOMEWORK JOURNAL

Men are born to succeed, not fail.

> Henry David Thoreau
> 1817-1862

Failure is a manmade condition. People are instinctually programmed to serve a greater purpose.

Parents must determine their passion and assist their children determining their passion early in their life. When you realize their purpose, *(notice I did not state determine your career or job)* their jobs and careers should match a person's purpose. Often people select jobs as to make a living to pay the bills without thought of whether the job/career fits their purpose. They then hate their profession.

Denzel Washington, Angeline Jolie, Ben Carson, and the A list goes on. Did you consider yourself in this list? Napoleon Hill states "the most important person you know is the person you are." The secret of true success in found within yourself. Therefore, the greatest feat is to find one's real self – to find individuality as you find yourself—to determine what your life's passion is.

People who chase their passions receive money. People who love what they do tend to immerse themselves into an activity they like causing them to produce great results. Most people who are experiencing trouble are experiencing a lifestyle or career they hate. Yes, you may be laid off or downsized and you had no control over this event. Maybe you did. Maybe your boss chose you to lay off or downsize because they did not feel your performance was stellar. Think about it! Could it be true?

I have always loved to troubleshoot finding and correcting problems. I created Hustle & TECHknow Preparatory High School as I discovered walking through many high schools within Detroit seventy-five percent of the students were female. It struck me odd that while the population of students is 50% female and 50% male, the typical high school was 75% female and 25% male. So I decided to create a school that catered to males but open to anyone. Hustle & TECHknow is a cyber school where students attend classes online with the assistance of an on-site coach. My students, former dropouts and juvenile delinquents, attended school every day. And when they did not, I called them to ask, "Where are you?"

Children love technology. Children love the computers. Children love videos. Children love video games and the interaction they bring. Children love music, audio and podcast. Children love mp3 players, IPods, and cell phones. The IPod soared off the sales charts due to Children. The video game industry is experiencing 18% growth due to Children. Cell phone companies are growing as more Children acquire cell phones. In this technology society, it is natural to create a cyber school full of computers so students are ready for today's global competition.

But more importantly they should have strong critical thinking skills. I am on the passion to create an education that makes them tech ready with critical thinking invention skills. One person and their passion can change the world. My passion will revolutionize public education forever. What is your passion? Can it change the world somehow? What is your child's passion? Help your children find their passion by finding your own passion.

COMPLETE #25 IN HOMEWORK JOURNAL

Cleanliness and order are not the matters of instinct; they are matters of education, and like most great things, you must cultivate a taste for them.

> Benjamin Disraeli
> 1804-1888

Children abhor cleanliness and order. Instinctively, nature is orderly chaos, but chaos nevertheless. Children must be instructed on how to clean and organize. This instruction should begin the day they learn to walk so after 10 years of practice cleanliness and order become second nature. Cleanliness and order are necessary to survive in this capitalistic world. Business people profit from organizing information into products, systems, processes and etc. Those who learn to organize at home learn to apply those skills to world. They also have an incredible advantage as the world rewards those who research, organize and distribute information, in either written or spoken form.

At Hustle & TECHknow, we had a student Richard who was impeccably dressed every day. He was always clean-shaven smelling fresh. He spoke well and walked with good posture. It was quite obvious his mother raised him well even though he tried so hard to be a thug. The students call him the "wanna be thug." He had a nice place to stay and his mother had invested in his grooming. Eventually one of the students told him it did not matter how many cases he caught – that is slang for court cases, he would never be a thug. Eventually he became a great student and he was one of our first graduates.

Many children do not develop an affinity for cleanliness. They write on furniture walls, anything without any regards for the destruction they are creating. They drop trash anywhere except the garbage cans. Some of our neighborhoods look like Beirut during the war because trash is located everywhere. Often children cannot play on playgrounds due to the large area covered by trash. We must socialize them to like cleanliness in our homes, our schools and in our communities. We must insist they clean up around them.

One caveat: Cleanliness for some is an excuse not to live and participate in some activities. Let you children live while teaching cleanliness. Some families will not let their children play in dirt, sand water etc. as their clothes will get dirty. They will. Just wash them.

This passage is to instill an environment of no trash, junk etc in neighborhoods. Many urban centers could be wholesome places to live if residents swept up trash, and eliminated graffiti.

Don't wait for everyone. Let the change begin with you. As a member of the parent group at Duke Ellington Conservatory of Music and Art, I led a team to repaint the school's outer doors, handrails as I could not take the filth another day. I also organized the sweeping, power washing of sidewalks and removal of trash weekly. Duke Ellington Conservatory of Music and Art was in a hardcore neighborhood. I was determined the school would not look that way.

COMPLETE #26 IN HOMEWORK JOURNAL

A Productive Education

Science is organized knowledge, Wisdom is organized life.

>Immanuel Kant
>1724-1804

"Wisdom is the highest and deepest degree of knowledge, insight and understanding, according to Cherie Canter – Scott Ph.D in her book, **Life is a game, these are the rules.** Wisdom does not come from age, but from a spiritual being higher than ourselves. It is the inner knowing that comes from the lessons we learn from life. It is the ability to sense information from pure observation. These lessons learned create an organized peaceful life, with stillness, free from fear, and judgment of others.

Many of us seek this organized peaceful life through the pursuit of money only to find it does not bring peace. This understanding is the beginning of wisdom. Yet, even when we find it, we fail to pass it along to our children under the guise they need to find their own way. They should but under our watchful protective guidance.

Those lessons learned should not be shared in a combative lecture but in loving every day conversation, discussions and sharing time. Often, those lessons will transcend into rules to protect your children. Don't be afraid to share that wisdom with them, but more importantly do not be afraid to live an organized life. With all the drama that occurs on television it may seem abnormal to have an organized peaceful life. While it is a rarity, it is not abnormal. It is the ultimate goal of life.

I realized one Christmas the $2000 dollars' worth of toys and stuff I bought my twins created angst for me and the twins. First, I saved money all year for Christmas. It is my favorite holiday and a big celebration for my family. Secondly, I hate to shop. Shopping absolutely drains my energy. So to buy those toys I am really wiped out. I then attempted to force Kevin and Karen to play with the toys creating frustration for them. They said they wanted those toys but in reality, they only played with the simple Lego blocks and china tea set. Based on that observation which is wisdom, I did three things. I asked them which do they prefer all the toys or a trip. At 5 years of age, they decided a trip. We have taken a Christmas/ Holiday vacation for 9 years, normally a cruise to relax. Everyone seems to love the result of that lesson including my son who introduced me to online shopping as he does most of his shopping online.

Secondly, every toy purchase was for simple toys related to school. I figure their play should become academic, causing me to read up on academic toys. I discovered board games to be great teachers of knowledge. Every Saturday until their 10th grade year we had Board Game Night at the Hills. They discontinued it only to pick it up again in 11th grade. I chuckled as they are 19 and for New Year's Eve 2012 we played games all night. First, Connect Four for 5 hours with 20 of their friends. It was grueling to watch them out strategize me. I guess 14 years of practice works. We then played video games. I could not keep up.

Playing games prepares students for science as it organizes their strategies and provides an environment to practice to experiment with those strategies.

Corporations are seeking students with a scientific background who can strategize, experiment and invent new things. Playing games prepares your children to love science and for employment in the 21st century. Give them both wisdom and science

COMPLETE #27 IN HOMEWORK JOURNAL

Education is the drawing out of soul.

>Ralph Waldo Emerson
>1803-1882
>Journal 20 Oct 1855

In today's society, people look upon individuals and judge their social standing, their worth, their economic class by the way they dress. We judge whether we want to associate, assist, or befriend based on their appearance. We judge whether they are worthy of our time.

While we see a person, and the image they are portraying, we never get the opportunity to "see" the real person. Even if we are in a long-term friendship, marriage, we may know lot about a person we will never know the real person. A person's appearance may reflect their inner spirit and their beliefs, but it is not the real person.

The real person is buried deep into their soul. Maybe we will see the real person or maybe not. We will only see this real person if we approved an individual without judgment. I met what I thought was the meanest lady ever. After I spoke to the old lady a few times, I discovered her gruff exterior was a cover for generous big-hearted loving person whom people have scammed often. The reason this lady was gruff was that someone scammed this lady of $150,000.

At Hustle & TECHknow Preparatory High Schools, I realized students are just like this lady. They often have tough hardcore thug ghetto appearances. While the world and other educational facilities dismiss these students as remedial drug dealers, their appearance is not the real person. I have discovered extremely bright, enthusiastic, loving, college preparatory students buried deep within their appearance. With lots of hug and a little encouragement, my "babies" rose to the occasion to grasp the education ring. What if I had judged my babies and provided a sour educational experience, would they have the ability to proceed to college? They would not. I am hoping I will find a Jay-Z or Ben Carson amongst our attendance rolls. In fact, I am looking for that student in every student.

Are you looking for the next great within your student? Who do you see?

Do you paint the vision to your children? I did every day of my children's life. I gave them the hope to become who they should be despite the poverty around us.

COMPLETE #28 IN HOMEWORK JOURNAL

Education should be a lifelong process, the formal period serving as a foundation on which life's structure may rest and rise.

>Robert Jackson (1892-1954)
>Supreme Court Justice

Education is not just showing up in school, it is an active participation in classroom activities, projects, homework and at home activities. Education is a lifelong process cemented with work completed in one's free time. Therefore, education is homework.

Homework is the time to review one's weaknesses and begin to improve on them. Homework is the time to review and rewrite class lecture notes. Homework is the time to memorize pertinent facts. Homework is the time to practice concepts. Homework is where the real education occurs.

Today's, educational facilities deny young people of real education when they do not assign homework daily. Homework is akin to the out of game activities of practice, weight training and good nutrition for a professional basketball player. It does not matter how talented the player is, if they neglect either one of the 3 activities they will not excel during the game. Neither will they earn the right to the championship game. Their body will not be fine-tuned and properly prepared for the rigors of running up and down the basketball court for 90 minutes.

Homework allows a student to practice ideas and concepts they learned in class. Homework allows a student to master a concept on their individual schedule whether it takes them 20 minutes or 2 hours. Homework solidifies study skills that are necessary to prepare for self-learning as a person will train and retrain for multiple careers, certification and licensure over today's longevity of life.

Since homework is education, do not allow your child to come home and fail to complete homework. Their grades in school will suffer as they are totally based on homework. Test, projects are driven by the homework. When students fail to complete their homework they cannot pass test nor complete excellent projects as they are lacking the necessary knowledge. But worse yet, they are deprived of real education.

If they say they do not have any homework, give them a research assignment. Or better, yet most textbooks in today's school have an online book that have assignments that the computer grades. Give them one of those assignments until they bring home homework.

Lastly, take the time to visit your student's classroom. Students will stretch the truth regarding school. Go see what chapters they are studying and when test are due to occur. The teacher will appreciate your involvement and you student will be so embarrassed they will attempt to complete their work to prevent you from returning to the classroom. I know this personally as I employ this strategy every marking period my students have been in school. They hate me visiting the school especially when they were in high school. Yes I visited high school. I love catching them in their stretched truths. Everyone comes clean when parents know the truth.

Parents need to visit more often during middle and high school as children have the freedom to go terribly wrong. What happens during this time can have a severe impact on their life. Our job is to keep them on track. The only way to know is to visit the school often. I visited high school monthly for 4 years developing strong relationships with teachers

COMPLETE #29 IN HOMEWORK JOURNAL

People who work sitting down get paid more than people who work standing up.

> Ogden Nash
> *US humorist & poet*
> *(1902 - 1971)*

As manufacturing is moving off the United States borders, we are becoming a society of designers, thinkers and processors. Most jobs require sitting behind a computer most of the day. Students learn this skill by sitting behind a computer monitor and digesting their information while manipulating word processing, spreadsheet, database and presentation software. The only way they can acquire that skill is to become immersed in virtual education.

Virtual education is instruction where the teacher provides course content through multimedia resources, the Internet, videoconferencing, etc. Students receive the content and communicate with the teacher via the same technologies.

There are various modes of virtual education:

Hypertext courses: Structured course material is used as in a conventional distance education program. However, all material is provided electronically and can be viewed over the internet.

Video-based courses are like face-to-face classroom courses, with a lecturer speaking and PowerPoint slides or online examples used for illustration. Video-streaming technologies is used. Students watch the video by means of freeware or plug-ins (e.g. Windows Media Player, RealPlayer).

Audio-based courses are similar but instead of moving pictures only the sound track of the lecturer is provided.

Animated courses: Enriching text-oriented or audio-based course material by animations is generally a good way of making the content and its appearance more interesting. Animations are created using Macromedia Flash or similar technologies.

Web-supported textbook courses are based on specific textbooks. Students read and reflect the chapters by themselves. Review questions, topics for discussion, exercises, case studies, etc. may be held in a chat room.

Virtual education is uni-directional meaning students complete assignments and discuss them with teacher or in chat rooms later. With programs such as Skype, Oovoo, webcams and microphones dropping in price, virtual education has become multidirectional with the student corresponding with the teacher who they are conversing over video. Homework assignments are normally submitted electronically, e.g. as an attachment to an e-mail. When help is needed, lecturers, tutors, or fellow students are available via electronic media.

According to Claire Raines, author of *Connecting Generations: The Sourcebook*, Millennials, those ages 13 to 23 years of age, learning preferences are teamwork, technology, structure, entertainment and experiential activities. These students are considered technical natives having been raised with cell phones, DVDs, and video game consoles since their birth. They are naturally technical savvy.

This population loves the excitement and thrill of video games. Millennials can be found manipulating video games — every day of the week for hours developing a skill of self-challenge Major game retailers, such as EB Games and GameStop, have followed these Millennials, even to locations within the inner city.

They even join together in informal clubs to compete. They read complicated gaming magazines to decipher how to cheat the game and game systems. Their curiosity, intensity and seriousness about their video games is refreshing. These students tend to have more success in a virtual oriented environment than in a traditional environment alone.

Most k-12 school districts offer students the ability to enroll in virtual classes at the school district's expense. Some have even incorporated it into the normal classroom. Everything that is offered in a traditional school building can be offered virtually. Even some coursework in subjects such as Mandarin Chinese, not offered in the building is offered virtually.

This virtual education teaches your student how to sit behind a computer and work as this is the reality for today's 21st century workforce

COMPLETE #30 IN HOMEWORK JOURNAL

The task of education is to make the individual so firm and sure that, as a whole being he can no longer be diverted from his path.

> Friedrich Nietzsche (1844-1900)

Most school systems are requiring the implementation of Educational Development Plans (EDP) for students prior to the completion of 8th grade.

An Education Development Plan documents an ongoing process in which a learner identifies both career goals and a plan of action to achieve them. The purpose of the EDP is to provide every student with a periodically updated and ongoing record of career planning that will guide in taking effective steps to enter a career of choice.

Each student first develops an EDP in middle school, stating an initial career goal and desired work and educational experiences. School counselors verify that EDPs reflect an individual career decision-making process based on career exploration, career assessment information, school performance, and expressed interests. School counselors also facilitate selection and enrollment into general courses and into specialized education and training related to the career pathway of choice indicated in the EDP.

Students update their EDP in the freshman year of high school as their interest may change and so will their career choice. Students will explore career choices in depth and determine what high school classes are necessary to prepare them for their post-secondary training and/or college education. Students will then update the EDP again in their junior year to insure they are on the right path to their success.

Often, students do not complete the Education Development Plan process or worse yet, schools do not initiate the process in the middle school grades. Students then attend high school and aimlessly wander through out their educational experience without a definite direction. Give them a pathway. Ensure they complete their Education Development Plan before thy complete 8th grade or in the first marking period of 9th Grade.

COMPLETE #31 IN HOMEWORK JOURNAL

A

Work

Ethic

The secret of joy in work is contained in one word – excellence. To know how to do something well is to enjoy it.

>Pearl Buck
>1892 – 1973 The Joy of Children – 1964

Young people of today have the mentality that just showing up at an activity they should be rewarded. While we are buying them multiple pairs of shoes, clothes and electronic devices, we forgot to teach them their reward is in the completion of a task to the best of their ability. We forgot to teach them that excellence is their reward, the ultimate reward. Excellence, once was the mantra of a job.

Young people learned this mentality from adults who are guaranteed pay raises for attending a job even if their performance is terrible. Whatever happened to pay based on merit, and performance. Whether their performance is mediocre or excellent their pay increase is the same. What incentive is there to provide excellence. We must instill excellence within the spirit of our young people. Excellence should be their driver.

While Hustle & TECHknow Preparatory High School is a ninth through twelfth grade high school classes are organized by performance on math exams. Students are ranked in this order as Eagles, Mustangs, Jaguars, Wolverines, Vipers or Bears.

Eagles are birds, which fly alone who set their own agenda. Birds, which are a replica of excellence. Mustangs are wild fast moving horses, which blaze their own trails. Jaguars are fast moving cats, which move by instinct and cannot be trained. Wolverines are fierce, fearless animals always on the move trying different ways to get the job done.   Vipers are sluggish but deadly animals, which are able to determine how much venom to inject into a predator to kill it.

Students hate the ranking, which is a public display of their test exams. However, they are motivated to study the subject material as they fully understand it determines their ranking in the school. Ranking occurs every two months. Ranking forces a student to embrace the values we adults have. In my home, I value education. My reward system rewards my children when they receive a GPA higher than 3.0 with money, electronics or trips. This forces them to consistently perform well academically.

COMPLETE #32 IN HOMEWORK JOURNAL

By the Work One Knows the Workmen

> Jean DeLa Fontaine
> (1621—1695)

The world does not demand that you become a physician, lawyer or merchant. It does demand you perform to the best of your ability.

Your reputation is created by your performance. It is all you have. Your reputation provides job opportunities, business and volunteer opportunities.

As a parent, I volunteered for Detroit Public Schools for five years. Increasing the MEAP test scores for Hanstein Elementary to 78.1% from 28.1% in reading, 69.1% from 39.1% in math respectively and then increased the MEAP access from 44% to 90%. I worked as if I were paid a consultant fee of $250.00 per hour.

Having transferred to a K-5 then a K-8 institution, it was normal to create a high school for dropouts and juvenile delinquents. That high school was created with a contract from Detroit Public Schools. I affection , named that high school, Hustle & TECHknow Preparatory High School to reflect the corporate hustle we must prepare our students for and the technology that is the driving force for corporate America. Our students' computer designs adorn our window front. Many visitors downtown stop and gaze at it.

COMPLETE #33 IN HOMEWORK JOURNAL

Opportunity is missed by most people because it is dressed in overalls and look like work.

       Thomas A. Edison
       (1847—1931)

Dreams and visions do not automatically become reality. They merely lay the foundation or plan to create the reality. Faith – the unquestioning belief that does not require proof -- is the power to propel the plan into action. Faith gives man the boldness to act upon the dream even when the current circumstances or living situations demand that the dream is a fantasy. The amount of faith a person possesses depends upon how a person sees themselves in relationship with God and humankind. If a person "sees" himself/herself as a failure, they have no faith to see their plan as a reality therefore they will not execute the plan. However, if a person "sees" himself/herself as a success, their plan becomes a reality so much as they will execute the plan. For when obstacles surround or block out a clear vision of the dream, faith empowers one.

Execution of a plan requires hard work and dedication necessary to complete the plan. Unfortunately, many people believe hoping, wishing, and dreaming causes a prayer and / or business to come into fruition. For that reason, 90% of start-up businesses fails within their first 5 years.

Plans and the execution of those plans through hard work is the only way to obtain success. Work creates the businesses. Work creates new ideas. Work creates money. "Work is the remedy – the magic potion," says Dennis Kimbro, author of What Makes the Great Great!

Young people of today want something for nothing. Because parents give them everything, they believe they are entitled to it due to their presence. Hustle & TECHknow Preparatory High rewards hard work. Trips, uniform distribution, even class assignments are based on work completion. Last year many students cried when they did not receive the coveted dress school uniform. While they attended often, they did not complete the work goal, which is to complete all assignments with a C average and 80% attendance. Parents must instill the work ethic into their children or they grow up to be spoiled rotten brats dependent upon other people.

COMPLETE #34 IN HOMEWORK JOURNAL

He that is busy is tempted by but one devil; he that is idle by a legion.

>   Thomas Fuller
>   1608 – 1661

Children must have activities, and chores to keep them mentally busy and to develop a strong value system. Chores should start as young as 4 years old. Thus, activity reduces their attempts into trouble and provides habits of the mind. Chores should be cutting grass, baby-sitting, running errands, planting flowers, or vegetable seeds, cleaning their room, washing dishes, grocery shopping, shoveling snow, etc.

Activities can be low cost or free such as walking, baseball, going to a dollar movie, baking cookies, reading a book, board games, cards etc. When children have too much idle time, they find activities to fill the time usually foolish troublesome activities. As parents, when children become older we must assist them in choosing their activities. Often what happens is that we believe they have adult brains to match their adult bodies. They do not. We must provide the activities until they are so exhausted from keeping up with us.

Yes, I know that is tiresome but the end result will be positively productive children. With that premise, the Hustle and TECHknow student is never finished with their work. If they master the concept, they move on to the next concept creating an intense internal competition against themselves and external activity.

COMPLETE #35 IN HOMEWORK JOURNAL

Time is Money

Benjamin Franklin

Everyone globally is seeking money. Money is valuable. It can determine the neighborhood you live in, the social circle you participate in, the school your children attend, the clothes you wear, the car you drive, your ranking in society. Money is very important. Despite its importance, money can be insured and replaced. But time, once it is gone, it is never replaced.

While money is important and valuable, time is the most precious resource. If one harnesses, organize and manage time, ideas germinate creating revenue and hence profits--- money. If time is wasted, nothing is gained. Time is a priceless commodity. Unfortunately, many people waste time seeking futile and dangerous methods to secure money. Some resort to criminal, deceptive and/ or manipulative behavior to secure money not realizing they are wasting time.

I realized students struggle not due to lack of money but rather improper usage of time. There are 24 hours in a day. Hustle & TECHknow Preparatory High School students attend school for 6 hours a day leaving 18 hours to work a job, study, sleep and eat. Students had the audacity to tell me they did not have time to study as they are struggling to live. When we showed them they could work a job 4 hours day and still have 14 hours left, they just could not comprehend as they do not really understand time management.

However, contrast their experience with the experience of Keisha, the mother of 2 children who organized her time extremely well. She dropped her children off at daycare and arrived at school every day by 8:50 am. If she was late, we worried as she was always in class. Keisha is now in college preparing to become a nurse.

In launching and organizing of Hustle & TECHknow Preparatory High School, my staff worked 65 hours per week to hone the process. It should have taken us 3 years to acquire computers, staff, and other resources given we lacked cash and staff. Yet it took 1 year. Time is the resource we should guard with our life.

COMPLETE #36 IN HOMEWORK JOURNAL

A

Fun

Playful

Adventure

The joy of the spirit is the measure of its power.

> Ninonde Lencios
> 1620-1705

Many people believe joy of the spirit is living an error free perfect life. Unfortunately, joy of the spirit has nothing to do with life circumstances. Joy of the spirit is an internal gratefulness of being able to breath one more day. Internal gratefulness for whatever situation life brings you. Life is 10% of circumstances that happen to you and 90% of how you feel and react to those circumstances.

Joy of the spirit will allow a distressed person to triumph over horrendous circumstances. Joy of the spirit gives an individual clarity to see opportunities that can be created to ease the financial struggle. Joy of the Spirit makes any task easier and more delightful.

Joy of the spirit is more commonly, known as enthusiasm. Enthusiasm begets enthusiasm. Enthusiasm turns an impossible task into a possibility. Enthusiasm turns a simple idea into a moneymaker. Enthusiasm invites peace and harmony.

Often, it is difficult to have enthusiasm in such a negative world. However, we have the ability to speak enthusiasm. When I greet people they ask " How are you?" Most people say "I'm fine." I usually state "I am fabulous, fantastic or magnificent." I am sometimes besieged with problems but the mention of those words psyche up my subconscious interjecting enthusiasm, which causes me to step up the pace and focus on something positive. Positivity fueled by enthusiasm create a power to supersede negative circumstances, events and activities of life.

COMPLETE #37 IN HOMEWORK JOURNAL

Always laugh when you can. It is cheap medicine.

> Lord Byron
> 1788-1824

Laughing and joy can cure a multitude of problems except those that are created by a physical chemical imbalance. Those imbalances are called by many names but the most prevalent in children is ADHD or Attention Deficit Hyperactivity Disorder and clinical depression. Both of these imbalances can be controlled with properly prescribed medication.

When children are under twelve, parents medicate them. When they become older, parents allow children to medicate themselves. Unfortunately, children either under medicate causing them to become terrors in school or they overdose themselves creating an enormous high and potential addiction. Parents must continually oversee their medication. As children are able to articulate the impact the medication has upon them, it is perfect time to schedule a meeting with your family physician to discuss the reduction, increase or change in the prescription. Sometimes the medication causes the student to become zombie like which is why they do not want to take the medicine.

Ralph is one of those students. His outburst would drive any normal teacher crazy. He stopped taking his medicine as his medication made him feel like a zombie. I convinced him to schedule a checkup. The physician reduced his dosage. His outburst were reduced significantly. Today, he is an extremely bright, hilarious and productive student.

COMPLETE #38 IN HOMEWORK JOURNAL

Life is either a daring adventure or nothing.

> Helen Keller
> 1880-1968 The Open Door

Children begin life with "an innate sense of wonder ready to explore their world. They are naturally curious ready to attempt anything once. They have no fear, no limits, no restraint. "An Adventure is any experience that takes you beyond your comfort level: any experience that causes the heart to beat with anticipation." Children lose this sense of adventure when they arrive in formal school only to reclaim it again in their teenage hood.

We categorize their adventure as craziness, foolishness. Yes, Children do some crazy deeds. When you can separate the consequences from the deed, their deeds are hilarious. They have a real sense of adventure.

As parents, it is our responsibility to massage and encourage this sense adventure in a positive manner. Travel is a positive way to massage that sense of adventure. At Hustle & TECHknow Preparatory High School, we capitalized on children's sense of adventure by going on field trips locally utilizing Detroit Department of Transportation. Given we are not sure when the bus will arrive or depart on time, we are unsure whether we will arrive at our intended location on time. Students learn how to navigate to field trips locations on the bus. They are accustomed to traveling by bus. Often, they returned to field trip locations in their personal time, meaning they learned and enjoyed the experience.

COMPLETE #39 IN HOMEWORK JOURNAL

It is only in adventure that some people succeed in knowing themselves - in finding themselves.

Andre Gide
1869 –1951

Adventures push individuals out of their comfort zones to sample new location, foods and cultures. We replace old favorites with new favorites. We redefine who we are by our adventures. We really begin to know ourselves. Adventures can be trips around the world or global journeys in our local community. Most metropolitan areas are comprised of various cultures and subcultures. Visit some of these cultural jewels and expose yourself and your children to another world right at home.

I discovered Michigan was the home of the Copper Rush. With the price of copper so enormously high, perhaps a short drive, approximately 8 hours into another world right in the state of Michigan, to visit a copper mine is in order. Or better yet, I saw the most unusual brown waterfall called Tahquamenon Falls. The water is brown due to the presence of copper.

Love sand beaches and amusement parks? You can get both in Santa Monica Pier's Park. Just 15 minutes from Los Angeles. There are 12 rides as well as miles of beaches. If you love to roller skate or skateboard you will be certainly at home. Not close to Michigan or California. How about a day trip to the wild walking nature trails to Cumberland Island in Georgia or the Okefenoke National Wildlife Refuge. You can explore swampland, and animals native to those swamplands. As my ancestors hailed from Georgia, I though was truly knowledge about Georgia until I visited the Refuge. I did not even know Georgia had swamplands like Florida. Or if you are a chicken lover than Buffalo is the place to be especially around Labor day where you can eat a portion of the 20 tons of Buffalo wings that are created to celebrate the Labor Day weekend. There are so many jewels across the country and even into Canada and Mexico. Have an adventure. Stomped for Ideas consult travel books, such as **1000 Places to See in the USA and Canada Before You Die** by Patricia Schultz or visit your local AAA and secure their travel handbooks. As you journey through out your community you may create enough information to create a book similar to the **Global Journeys of Metro Detroit** created by Helen Love. Global Journeys has been my field trip bible I never leave home without.

COMPLETE #40 IN HOMEWORK JOURNAL

Certainly, travel is more than the seeing of sights; it is a change that goes on, deep and permanent in the ideas of the living.

Miriam Beard

High School and college admissions are based on grade point averages and student's performance on standardized test such as the ACT or SAT. Many parents invest money in sophisticated desktop/ laptop computers to give their children access to the worldwide web. Some establish home offices, libraries and structured areas to encourage daily homework and studying as many believe constant studying and attention to homework will give their students impeccable credentials. To a certain extent, those parents are correct. Homework and study skills lay the basic foundation for school success as high grade point averages flow from high-test scores.

Memory skills and repetition is the key to high grade point averages; however, they are not the key to brilliance on standardized test. Standardized test, such as California Achievement Test (CAT), Scholastic Aptitude Test (SAT), American College Test (ACT), assumes students are exposed to different cultures, climates, countries and experiences at least 10 times before reaching 10th grade. Students who perform the best on standardized test have exposure to diverse experiences. What better way to gain this exposure than a vacation to another city, state, country or continent!!!!!

Wealthy families have always known that trips, getaways and vacations are the secret to grooming brilliant students. "Family vacations are going hard core. Some parents are loading their kids onto 12-hour flights to sub-Saharan Africa or Asia. Others are packing itineraries with extreme experiences, sending their children rocketing down zip lines in the jungle or bicycling through rice paddies in Thailand. They are being inspired by -- or some say, competing with --

other parents who are busy padding out their children's passports." Power Trips for Tots *(Wall Street Journal April 21, 2007.)* Family vacations are an opportunity for students to apply all their classroom knowledge quickly. The average vacation is three to seven days. While some wealthy families are known to vacation up to 45 days on multiple continents, most families are on a limited timeframe requiring them to make quick decisions regarding currency exchange, climate differences, navigation of city, etc.

These decisions while extremely practical require the use of mathematics, science, geography, social studies and reading. Unconsciously, students are immersed into lessons fueled by sheer excitement and curiosity. Children learn lessons at a faster pace with hands on experience. A train trip to an Indian Reservation in Arizona/ New Mexico really solidifies a lesson on Native American History. A field trip to the any continent solidifies lessons in currency exchange, physics, climate, geography, history, art and music culture.

For that reason, Uplift, Inc. created a program entitled Exposures & Explorations. Hustle & TECHknow Preparatory High School students were the first participants. They visited museums, events such as Cinco De Mayo. They visited the North American Auto Show, cultural exchanges with different cultures. For the end of the year, they visited Chicago by train to see The Color Purple the musical. They basked in the luxury of the Wyndham Hotel. Their lives were changed forever.

COMPLETE #41 IN HOMEWORK JOURNAL

...Adventure in flying, in world travel, in business and even close at hand.... Adventure is a state of mind and spirit.

                        Jacqueline Cochran
                        1910 - 1980

Adventure is a state of mind and spirit that comes from like innocence that every activity is a learning opportunity and time to explore. Having served as the neighborhood mom where everyone visits, something simple as playing board games. While I am a video game junkie, I played board games every Saturday Night with my children, It is not uncommon to find 8 to 12 children visiting. Board games are a great source for children to learn critical thinking, strategy and social skills. Try a new game Fluke – the wealth building game of accidental inventions

The spirit of adventure comes from having child- like innocence. Everyone has somewhere deep within. We realized at Hustle & TECHknow Preparatory High School even big kids have it, too.

We organize special events to celebrate holidays monthly. Everyone participates. While the events are not that grand, the giggles and high fives abound we have learned to create. We particularly realized this when we celebrated St. Patrick's Day. We had only 1 Irish student, yet the luck of the Irish, the Kelly green beads and leprechaun hats along with the Irish meal of Corned beef, potatoes cabbage and bread pudding had everyone feeling quite grand!!!!!

COMPLETE #42 IN HOMEWORK JOURNAL

Tips for Emotionally Healthy Successful Students

Homework Journal

This appendix is a workbook journal to store your thoughts in one place. You can tear the pages and staple the pages down the left hand side of the page. Write notes for each section.

Journaling is often considered an individual activity. However, everyone who has teenagers are being driven crazy equally. Turn journaling into a group social activity. Schedule a discussion club. Add food and fun.

Take the **Behavior Quiz** below to see if your child is too much of a risk taker. Check the statements that apply to your child.

BEHAVIOR QUIZ

- ☐ Are you visiting teachers often due to your child's behavior?
- ☐ Has your child experienced a drop in academic performance?
- ☐ Does your child struggle with basic family rules and expectations?
- ☐ Has your child ever been suspended, expelled from school?
- ☐ Is your child verbally abusive?
- ☐ Does your child associate with a bad peer group?
- ☐ Has your child lost interest in former activities, hobbies or sports?
- ☐ Do you have difficulty getting your child to do simple household chores?
- ☐ Has your child had problems with the law?
- ☐ Do you find yourself picking your words carefully when speaking to your child to avoid a verbal attack?

- Are you worried that your child may not finish high school?
- Does your child seem depressed/ withdrawn?
- Has your child's appearance and/ or personal hygiene changed?
- Does your child ever display violent behavior?
- Is your child manipulative and/or deceitful?
- Does your child seem to demonstrate a lack of motivation?
- Do you suspect that your child sometimes lies or is dishonest with you?
- Are you concerned that your child may be sexually promiscuous?
- Has your child ever displayed any evidence of suicide ideation?
- Do you suspect at times you have had other valuables stolen from your home?
- Does your child's behavior concern for your safety?
- Is your child angry or display temper outbursts?
- Does your child seem to lack self-esteem and self-worth?
- Do you have a lack of trust with your child?
- Does your child have problems with authority?
- Does your child engage in activities you don't approve of?
- Do you think your child is possibly using or experimenting with drugs/alcohol?
- Are you concerned about your child 's well-being and their future?
- Does your child seem to constantly be in opposition to your family values?
- No matter what rules and consequences are established, does your child defy them?
- Are you exhausted and worn out from your child's defiant and/or destructive behavior and choices?
- When dealing with your child, do you often feel that you are powerless?
- Is your child on probation?

If you answered *yes* to seven or more of the above questions, your child is headed for trouble. Read K.I.S.S. Begins At Home to determine intervention strategies.

If you answered *yes* to eleven or more of the above questions, your child is in trouble K.I.S.S. Begins At Home to determine rescue strategies.

A Loving Atmosphere

#1   *Love the answer to the problem of human existence.*

Erich Fromm 1900-1980
The Art of Loving 2.1 (1956)

Get to know your children. Give them a copy of **The Favorites List**. Have them complete every line and give the copy back to you. Memorize their favorites you will need them later in the book. At the conclusion of the list completion, say "I love you!!!!" to your child.

Say, *"I love you!!!"* to you child for 1 week every morning. Observe and note your expression and their response.

1.	Favorite color	_____
2.	Lucky number	_____
3.	Favorite season	_____
4.	Favorite time of day	_____
5.	Favorite holiday	_____
6.	Favorite hobby	_____
7.	Favorite sports activity	_____
8.	Favorite type of jewelry	_____
9.	Silver, gold or platinum	_____
10.	Preferred style of dress	_____
11.	Favorite part of body	_____

12.	Favorite outfit	_____
13.	Lucky charm	_____
14.	Favorite food	_____
15.	Favorite vegetable	_____
16.	Favorite fruit	_____
17.	Favorite cookie	_____
18.	Favorite ice cream	_____
19.	Favorite chocolate	_____
20.	Favorite candy	_____
21.	Favorite snack food	_____
22.	Favorite soft drink	_____
23.	Favorite fast food joint	_____
24.	Favorite restaurant (cheap)	_____
25.	Favorite restaurant (expensive)	_____
26.	Favorite meal	_____
27.	Favorite website	_____
28.	Favorite TV show (current)	_____
29.	Favorite TV show (old)	_____
30.	Favorite reality show	_____
31.	Favorite game show	_____
32.	Favorite TV channel	_____
33.	Favorite movie of all time	_____
34.	Favorite	_____

	adventure movie	
35.	Favorite action movie	_____
36.	Favorite animated movie	_____
37.	Favorite comedy movie	_____
38.	Favorite Broadway play	_____
39.	Favorite musical	_____
40.	Favorite actor (living)	_____
41.	Favorite actor (of any era)	_____
42.	Favorite actress(living)	_____
43.	Favorite actress(of any era)	_____
44.	Favorite fictional character	_____
45.	Favorite animated character	_____
46.	Favorite comic strip	_____
47.	Favorite comic book	_____
48.	Favorite TV cartoon	_____
49.	Favorite TV cartoon character	_____
50.	Favorite type of music	_____
51.	Favorite band	_____
52.	Favorite artist	_____
53.	Favorite type of music	_____
54.	Favorite dance tune	_____

55.	Favorite romantic song	_____
56.	Favorite chillin' song	_____
57.	Favorite song	_____
58.	Favorite role model (living)	_____
59.	Favorite role model (dead)	_____
60.	Favorite role model (fictional)	_____
61.	Favorite historical personality	_____
62.	Favorite sports (to watch)	_____
63.	Favorite athlete	_____
64.	Favorite sports team	_____
65.	Favorite board game	_____
66.	Favorite card game	_____
67.	Favorite book (fiction)	_____
68.	Favorite book (nonfiction)	_____
69.	Favorite fairy tale	_____
70.	Favorite children's book	_____
71.	Favorite religious passage	_____
72.	Favorite saying	_____
73.	Favorite poem	_____
74.	Favorite way to relax	_____
75.	Favorite to get energized	_____
76.	Favorite store	_____

77.	Favorite shopping mall	_____
78.	Favorite city	_____
79.	Favorite country	_____
80.	Favorite way to spend lazy day	_____
81.	Favorite perfume/cologne	_____
82.	Best gift ever received	_____

"I Love You" Observation

_____
_____
_____
_____
_____
_____
_____
_____
_____
_____
_____
_____
_____
_____
_____
_____
_____
_____
_____
_____
_____

#2 *There is only one thing that has power and that is love.*

Alan Paton 1903-1988
Cry the Beloved Country (1948)

SMILE at you child for 1 week every time you physically see your child.

Observe and note your expression and their response.

Having difficulty smiling for an entire week? Here is some extra homework to prepare you for your smile fest.

Make faces in the mirror	Jump on the bed
Bake cookies	Dance to loud music
Visit a playground	Watch cartoons
Listen to a well-known comedian -	Visit a pet store

Write down your feelings about the extra homework assignments when they are complete.

_____
_____
_____
_____
_____
_____
_____
_____
_____
_____
_____
_____
_____
_____
_____
_____
_____
_____
_____
_____
_____
_____
_____
_____
_____
_____
_____
_____

#3 *Human Nature is so constructed that it gives affection most readily to those who seem least to demand it.*

Bertrand Russell (1872-1970)
The Conquest of Happiness 12, 1930

Hug your child 4 times a day for 1 week. Observe and note your expression and their response.

_____
_____
_____
_____
_____
_____
_____
_____
_____
_____
_____
_____
_____
_____
_____
_____
_____
_____
_____
_____
_____
_____
_____
_____
_____

#4 *Show Kindness to your Parents.*

Muhammad (A.D. 570-632)
Quran 6.151

Give Lip Kisses to your child for 1 week. Observe and note your expression and their response.

_____
_____
_____
_____
_____
_____
_____
_____
_____
_____

Give Kisses – Hershey's Chocolate Kisses in a decorative bag/ container to your child every day for 1 week. Place some of these Kisses in a candy jar as well all throughout the house. Observe and note your expression and their response.

_____
_____
_____
_____
_____
_____
_____
_____
_____
_____
_____

A Rock Foundation

#5 *A home is not a mere transient shelter; its essence lies in its permanence's, in its capacity for accretion and solidification.*

H. L. Mencken (1880---1924)
"On Living in Baltimore"
Prejudices: Faith Series 1924

Reflect: Write down all the addresses you have had in the past 17 years. Name your child's friends at each address.

_____
_____
_____
_____
_____
_____
_____
_____
_____
_____
_____
_____
_____
_____
_____
_____
_____
_____
_____
_____
_____
_____
_____
_____
_____

#6 *I've never been poor only broke. Being poor is a frame of mind. Being broke is only a temporary situation.*

Mike Todd (1909—1958)
Death of a Showman,
Newsweek 31 March 1958

Are You Poor?

1. Are your friends' constant complainers?
2. Do you complain about the lack of opportunity?
3. Do you lack goals with forward direction?
4. Do you live from paycheck to paycheck?
5. Do you have any savings or investments?
6. Do you constantly worry about your finances?
7. Do you pamper physical items, such as furniture as if you will never get any other items?
8. Do you shop for luxuries before paying your bills?
9. Do you spend the bulk of your money on consumable items, such as clothes?
10. Is your car payment greater than your house payment?

If you answered **yes** to two or more of these questions, **YOU ARE POOR!**

View the movie **The Secret** at www.secret.tv. Write down every negative thought as it occurs for one week. Write a positive thought immediately.

 # 7 *A man is rich whose income is larger than his expenses and he is poor if his expenses are greater than his income.*
La Bruyere (1645 – 1696)
"Of Gifts of Fortune" (49) The Characters 1688

Complete budget. Determine what income is left at the end of each month. Establish a saving/ investment plan. If you have nothing leftover, Please explain why. Look to reduce some expenses.

Home Budget Sheet

Income	$_____
Expenses:	
Housing Rent	$_____
Car payment	$_____
Insurance	$_____
Parking	$_____
Electric/Gas	$_____
Water	$_____
Phones	$_____
Food	$_____
Entertainment	$_____
Beauty	$_____
Other	$_____
Total Expenses	$_____
Money Left Over	$_____

Monthly Savings $_____

If you have nothing leftover, Please explain why. Look to reduce some expenses.

_____
_____
_____
_____
_____
_____
_____
_____
_____
_____
_____
_____
_____
_____
_____
_____
_____
_____
_____
_____
_____
_____
_____
_____
_____
_____
_____
_____
_____
_____
_____
_____

#8 *When you are poor, you grow up fast.*

Billie Holiday (1915 -1959)
Lady Sings the Blues, 1956

Relive your innocence. Arrange a childish activity with your child.

Fishing	Skating	Crafts
Model Cars	Model Airplanes	Tennis
Basketball	Bike Riding	Dancing
Football	Video Games	Catch
Jump Rope	Camping	Baseball
Crocheting	Knitting	

Detail your experience here:

_____
_____
_____
_____
_____
_____
_____
_____
_____
_____
_____
_____
_____
_____
_____
_____
_____
_____
_____

A Positive Thought

#9 *Man is not the creature of circumstance, circumstance are the creatures of men. We are free agents, and man is more powerful than matter.*

Benjamin Disraeli (1804—1881)
Vivian Grey 6,7 1826

Reflect on your thoughts. What are you thinking right now? Write them down. Are they thoughts of scarcity or abundance? Write down the opposite thought.

#10 *Everything you can imagine is real*

Pablo Picasso (1881- 1973)

What do you think you can do? Describe your plans

_____
_____
_____
_____
_____
_____
_____
_____
_____
_____
_____
_____
_____
_____
_____
_____
_____
_____
_____
_____
_____
_____
_____
_____
_____
_____
_____
_____
_____
_____
_____

#11 *Death and life are in the power of the tongue.*

    Proverbs 18:21
    The Bible (King James Version)

Give your children a compliment every day for 21 days. Record their response.

_____
_____
_____
_____
_____
_____
_____
_____
_____
_____
_____
_____
_____
_____
_____
_____
_____
_____
_____
_____
_____
_____
_____
_____
_____
_____
_____
_____
_____

#12 *Self-control and self-esteem vary directly. The more self-esteem a person has, the greater, as a rule, is his desire, and his ability to control himself.*

Thomas S. Szasz (1920 --)
Control and Self Control Heresies, 1976

See how much self-esteem you possess. Answer these questions honestly in the **SELF ESTEEM QUIZ**.

SELF ESTEEM QUIZ

Circle numbers 1-4 that honestly reflect your pattern of operation.

1-Almost Never   2-Occasionally   3-Frequently   4-Almost all the time

1. Do you surround yourself with positive people?
2. Do you love your work?
3. Do you love yourself when things go wrong?
4. Are you your own best friend when you make a mistake or blow it?
5. Do you matter to others?
6. Do you acknowledge your own accomplishments?
7. Do you enjoy learning new things?
8. Are you healthy?
9. Have you had any expert "image" consultations?
10. Do you surround yourself with people you admire?

11. Do you have a trusted friend or colleague that you can let your hair down with?

12. Are you able to ask for something when you want it?

13. When you are rejected, do you take it personally?

14. Do you understand yourself when others don't?

15. Can you laugh at yourself?

16. Are you "on track" for you?

17. Do others enjoy being around you?

18. Do you forgive yourself for mistakes that you make?

19. When you have failed at something, can you still be around others?

20. Are you true to you?

Total all numbers. **This is your final score**.

SCORE

72 – 80 points
BRAVO!!! You are an accomplished person, who has a sense of who you are. You have learned how to get, keep and grow self - esteem.

61-71 points
IMPRESSIVE!!! You have a strong sense of self – esteem, which is illustrated in your leadership abilities to achieve your dreams. Your sense of self is definitely a key ingredient to move you to be the greatest success ever.

50-60 points
AVERAGE!!! Your self - esteem level is average meaning you will yield average returns in achieving your dream.

Perhaps it is time for you to stretch yourself – to learn something new about yourself and your chosen career passion.

39-49 points
SHAKY!!! Your self - esteem level waivers – one moment you feel you can conquer the world the next moment you feel you can't do anything right. Let's stabilize your self esteem.

Below 38
YIKES!!! Major self - esteem surgery is needed. You seek negative people and situations to confirm your low self-esteem. Read on to quickly repair yourself as "*no one can make you feel inferior without your permission.*" (Eleanor Roosevelt)

#13 *Success is the ability to go from one failure to another with no loss of enthusiasm.*

Sir Winston Churchill (1874—1965)

Review a failure. What did you learn? Could you use it for another opportunity?

A Listening Ear

#14 *Nothing has a stronger influence psychologically on their environment and especially on their children than the unlived life of the parent*

Carl Jung (1881- 1973)

Are you living the life you desire? _____ If not, what is that life? What can you do to live that life today?

_____
_____
_____
_____
_____
_____
_____
_____
_____
_____
_____
_____
_____
_____
_____
_____
_____
_____
_____
_____
_____
_____
_____
_____
_____
_____

#15 *Children have never been very good at listening to their elders, but they have never failed to imitate them.*

James Baldwin (1881- 1973)

Take Quiz and Score

Lifestyle Funk Quiz

1. Your alarm clock on buzzes at 5:30 am. Do you?:

    a) Jump out of bed excited to face the day.
    b) Slowly get out of bed, shower, dress arriving 10 - 20 minutes late
    c) Continually hit the snooze button until it is 7:00 knowing you are 40 minutes from your job, which begins at 8:00 am

2. Your average workday:

    a) Flies by with you enjoying every minute.
    b) Crawls at a snail's pace.
    c) **Is just that—another day.**

3. Your work:

    a) Excites you to the point of creating work holism.
    b) Bores you to death.
    c) Leaves you drained at the end of the day.

4. My job/ my business:

    a) Is my dream
    b) Allows me to obtain the finer things in life.
    c) Is the means to a paycheck

5. My career/ my business:

a) Is growing upwardly by leaps and bounds.
   b) Grows laterally as I pick up different.
   c) Has remained the same.

6. When you arrive at home you:

   a) Play with the kids enthusiastically
   b) Eat dinner and go to sleep
   c) Yell at the kids.

7. Your stresses causes you to:

   a) Exercise for relief.
   b) Drink alcohol to relieve yourself.
   c) Beat your wife and kids.

8. You are addicted to:

   a) Alcohol, illegal drugs, prescribed pharmaceuticals
   b) Food, sex, shopping
   c) Beating your spouse and kids.

9. You are:

   a) Calm and peaceful.
   b) Bored.
   c) Frustrated.

10. **Your greatest complaint is:**

    a) "I need more social time."
    b) "I have too many bills."
    c) "I lack money."

Score
5 points for each C answer, 3 points for each B answer, 1 point for each A answer

50-36 Points
You are in a **LIFESTYLE FUNK**. You need to discover who you really are and what passion drives you.

35-25 Points

You are on the Verge of **LIFESTYLE FUNK**. Your lifestyle may excite you but other external circumstances frustrate you. You need to discover if you truly love your current passion rather than activities to hide your pain.

24 - Below Points
Congratulations! You are living a **DREAM** lifestyle.

If you had millions of dollars, what would you do to occupy yourself? This is your passion. How can you earn a living with this passion today

_____
_____
_____
_____
_____
_____
_____
_____
_____
_____
_____
_____
_____
_____
_____

#16 *When people talk, listen completely. Most people never listen.*

Ernest Hemingway (1899-1961)

Schedule at least 3 hours of free time with your children. Observe if they talk to you about their life. Record the conversation here:

___

#17 *The character of a man is known from his conversations.*

Menander (342 BC – 291 BC)

Listen to your coworkers. What did you learn from them?

_____
_____
_____
_____
_____
_____
_____
_____
_____
_____
_____
_____
_____
_____
_____
_____
_____
_____
_____
_____
_____
_____
_____
_____
_____
_____
_____
_____

A Structured Discipline

#18 *A Man's Character is his Fate.*
Heraclitus
540 BC – 480 BC On the Universe

What values drive you? Give an example of each value.

Value	Example of Value In Action
1 _____	_____
2 _____	_____
3 _____	_____
4 _____	_____
5 _____	_____
6 _____	_____
7 _____	_____

#19 *The thing that impresses me the most about America is the way parents obey their children.*

King Edward VIII (1884 – 1972)

Recall an incident where you followed your child's demands. How do you feel about the outcome? Recall an incident when you resisted their tantrum. How did you feel?

#20 *There is a measure in everything. There are fixed limits beyond which and short of which right cannot find a resting place.*

Horace
Roman lyric poet & satirist (65 BC - 8 BC)

Listen to your conversation with your children. It is apparent what you consider important for them. Write those items here.

_____
_____
_____
_____
_____
_____
_____
_____
_____
_____
_____
_____
_____
_____
_____
_____
_____
_____
_____
_____
_____
_____
_____
_____
_____

#21 *Right discipline consists, not in external compulsion, but in habits of mind, which lead spontaneously to desirable rather than undesirable activities.*

Bertrand Russell (1872-1970)
On Education: Especially in Early Childhood

Write down the rules of your house. Post them on the refrigerator or message for your family.

#22 *Nothing is stronger than habits*

Ovid 43BC – 17AD
Ars Amatoria

Examine your habits. List positive habits. List negative habits. Write a plan to strengthen the positive and attempt to change the negative

Positive Habits   **Negative Habits**

1 _____   _____
2 _____   _____
3 _____   _____
4 _____   _____
5 _____   _____

_____
_____
_____
_____
_____
_____
_____
_____
_____
_____
_____
_____
_____
_____
_____
_____
_____

#23 *A Goal Without a Plan is Just a Wish.*

Antoine de Saint – Exypery
1900—1944

Complete your 101 Goal list. Have your children complete their own goal list.

101 Goal list

1. _____ 2. _____
3. _____ 4. _____
5. _____ 6. _____
7. _____ 8. _____
9. _____ 10. _____
11. _____ 12. _____
13. _____ 14. _____
15. _____ 16. _____
17. _____ 18. _____
19. _____ 20. _____
21. _____ 22. _____
23. _____ 24. _____
25. _____ 26. _____
27. _____ 28. _____
29. _____ 30. _____
31. _____ 32. _____

33. _____	34. _____
35. _____	36. _____
37. _____	38. _____
39. _____	40. _____
41. _____	42. _____
43. _____	44. _____
45. _____	46. _____
47. _____	48. _____
49. _____	50. _____
51. _____	52. _____
53. _____	54. _____
55. _____	56. _____
57. _____	58. _____
59. _____	60. _____
61. _____	62. _____
63. _____	64. _____
65. _____	66. _____
67. _____	68. _____
69. _____	70. _____
71. _____	72. _____
73. _____	74. _____
75. _____	76. _____
77. _____	78. _____
79. _____	80. _____

81._____	82._____
83._____	84._____
85._____	86._____
87._____	88._____
89._____	90._____
91._____	92._____
93._____	94._____
95._____	96._____
97._____	98._____
99._____	100. _____
101. _____	

#24 He who every morning plans the transaction of the day and follow out that plan, carries a thread that will guide him through the maze of the most busy life. But where no plan is laid, where the disposal of time is surrendered merely to the chance of incidence, chaos will soon reign.

Victor Hugo 1802—1885

Identify a short-term goal (6 months or less) on the 101-goal list. For 1 week, every evening reflect on the day's activities and write a plan for each day on how to achieve that goal.

Day of Week	Goal for Today
Sunday	_____
Monday	_____
Tuesday	_____
Wednesday	_____
Thursday	_____
Friday	_____
Saturday	_____

#25 *Men are born to succeed, not fail.*

Henry David Thoreau 1817-1862

If you had a million dollars what thing would you love to do more than anything?

#26 *Cleanliness and order are not the matters of instinct; they are matters of education, and like most great things, you must cultivate a taste for them.*

Benjamin Disraeli
1804-1888

Have your children reorganize your house. Begin with their bedrooms and move to each room until the house is organized. If your house is clean and organized then organize either a cleanup of your community park, school yard etc. Detail your experience here.

_____
_____
_____
_____
_____
_____
_____
_____
_____
_____
_____
_____
_____
_____
_____
_____
_____
_____
_____
_____
_____
_____
_____
_____
_____
_____

A Productive Education

#27 *Science is organized knowledge, Wisdom is organized life.*

Immanuel Kant
1724-1804

Determine what would create a peaceful organized life. Do not be afraid to eliminate some of the modern traditions that cause great stress.

#28 *Education is the drawing out of soul.*

Ralph Waldo Emerson 1803-1882
Journal 20 Oct 1855

Look at your own children. Who do you see? List both positive and negative traits for your children.

#29 *Education should be a lifelong process, the formal period serving as a foundation on which life's structure may rest and rise.*

Robert Jackson (1892-1954)
Supreme Court Justice

Review and Track homework progress for 3 weeks. Quiz them yourself to see if they are retaining the material.

	Assignment	**Grade**
English	_____	_____
Math	_____	_____
Science	_____	_____
Social Studies	_____	_____
Homework	_____	_____
Elective	_____	_____
Elective	_____	_____

	Assignment	Grade
English	_____	_____
Math	_____	_____
Science	_____	_____
Social Studies	_____	_____
Homework	_____	_____
Elective	_____	_____
Elective	_____	_____

	Assignment	Grade
English	_____	_____
Math	_____	_____
Science	_____	_____
Social Studies	_____	_____
Homework	_____	_____
Elective	_____	_____
Elective	_____	_____

#30 *People who work sitting down get paid more than people who work standing up.*

Ogden Nash
US humorist & poet (1902 - 1971)

Contact your school district and discover who do they recommended as a virtual course provider. Enroll your child in a virtual course. Track their performance. Do they perform better, faster? Detail your experience here.

#31 *The task of education is to make the individual so firm and sure that, as a whole being he can no longer be diverted from his path.*

Friedrich Nietzsche (1844-1900)

Contact your Child's school and ask for a copy of the child's Educational Development Plan. Write down their career choice, where they plan on attending their post-secondary training and how they plan on paying for it. If there is no EDP, Complete the one below. Read **Escape to College**

Educational Development Plan

Child #1
Name_____
Grade _____

Career Pathway
_____

Career Choices_____

ACT Test dates	Scores
_____	_____
_____	_____
_____	_____

Post-Secondary Training Options
_____
_____
_____

Scholarship Opportunities
_____   Deadline _____
_____   Deadline _____
_____   Deadline _____

Educational Development Plan

Child #2
Name_____
Grade _____

Career Pathway
_____

Career Choices_____

ACT Test dates   Scores

_____   _____
_____   _____
_____   _____

Post-Secondary Training Options
_____
_____
_____

Scholarship Opportunities
_____   Deadline _____
_____   Deadline _____
_____   Deadline _____

A Work Ethic

#32 *The secret of joy in work is contained in one word – excellence. To know how to do something well is to enjoy it.*

Pearl Buck 1892 – 1973
The Joy of Children – 1964

Name a job (project) volunteer or earning where you gave your best ability ever.

_____
_____
_____
_____
_____
_____
_____
_____
_____
_____
_____
_____
_____
_____
_____
_____
_____
_____
_____
_____
_____
_____
_____
_____
_____

#33 *By the Work one Knows the Workmen*

Jean DeLa Fontaine
(1621—1695)

What does your work state about you? Excellence, mediocre, poor. Reflect on an example and explain.

#34 *Opportunity is missed by most people because it is dressed in overalls and look like work.*

Thomas A. Edison (1847—1931)

Write down avenues of work you absolutely abhor but is necessary to achieve your goal. Have your (children) do the same.

_____
_____
_____
_____
_____
_____
_____
_____
_____
_____
_____
_____
_____
_____
_____
_____
_____
_____
_____
_____
_____
_____
_____
_____
_____
_____
_____
_____

#35 *He that is busy is tempted by but one devil; he that is idle by a legion.*

Thomas Fuller
1608 – 1661

Create a child-centric calendar for the next month. Include fun activities, chores, homework time studying and just free time. Utilize Google calendar. Events can be color coded. Write down suggestions here.

#36 *Time is Money*

Benjamin Franklin

Fill in the daily activities schedule on your calendar. How much time do your children have each day for extra activities? Fill in the time. How much time do your children have for homework and extra activities? Write down why they have so much time and what they do with the time.

___

A Fun Playful Adventure

#37 *The joy of the spirit is the measure of its power.*

Ninonde Lencios
1620-1705

When everything is going wrong, speak positive statements such as;

> I am Fabulous
> I am fantastic
> I am wealthy
> I am happy
> I am ok

Commit to saying this statement for 1 month. Write a description of how you feel after you continually say these statements. Write a description of how events changed if they changed.

_____
_____
_____
_____
_____
_____
_____
_____
_____
_____
_____
_____
_____
_____
_____

#38 *Always laugh when you can. It is cheap medicine.*

Lord Byron
1788-1824

Schedule a physical checkup for your student. Discuss any abnormalities with your physician. Develop a plan of action to resolving those abnormalities. Describe the results of your checkup. Did it help calm your student? And how?

#39 *Life is either a daring adventure or nothing.*

Helen Keller
1880-1968 The Open Door

Research every day adventures in your home city you have not visited before or in long time. List them here. Put them on your monthly schedule to visit them with your children. Record your experiences here.

Daring Adventure #1
_____
_____
_____
_____

Daring Adventure #2
_____
_____
_____
_____

Daring Adventure #3
_____
_____
_____
_____

Daring Adventure #4
_____
_____
_____
_____

Daring Adventure #5
_____
_____
_____
_____

#40 *It is only in adventure that some people succeed in knowing themselves - in finding themselves.*

Andre Gide
1869 –1951

Research and compile a list of jewels in your hometown. Visit as many as you can. Detail your experience here.

Hometown Adventure Jewels

1. _____
2. _____
3. _____
4. _____
5. _____
6. _____
7. _____
8. _____
9. _____
10. _____

11. _____
12. _____
13. _____
14. _____
15. _____
16. _____
17. _____
18. _____
19. _____
20. _____

#41 *Certainly, travel is more than the seeing of sights; it is a change that goes on, deep and permanent in the ideas of the living.*

Miriam Beard

Research various travel sites. Select a destination for a short-term (3-5 day) trip. Compare cost here.

Website _____

Location	Transport Cost	Lodging Cost (Hotel/ Cruise)	Total Entertain* Cost
_____	_____	_____	_____
_____	_____	_____	_____
_____	_____	_____	_____
_____	_____	_____	_____
_____	_____	_____	_____
_____	_____	_____	_____

*****Total Entertainment Cost**

Theater Shows	Amusement Park Fees	Shopping	Dining	Local Transport
_____	_____	_____	_____	_____
_____	_____	_____	_____	_____
_____	_____	_____	_____	_____
_____	_____	_____	_____	_____
_____	_____	_____	_____	_____

#42 *...Adventure in flying, in world travel, in business and even close at hand.... Adventure is a state of mind and spirit.*

Jacqueline Cochran
1910 – 1980

Play the Favorites Guessing Game as adapted from **Love, The Course They Forgot to Teach you in School** by Greg J.P. Godek with your children. Give each back the list of favorites you collected at the beginning of this book. Give each child 10 Hershey Kisses. If you guess their favorites correctly, they give you a Hershey kiss. The goal of the game is that you will possess each child's ten kisses at the end. If you end the Favorites Guessing Game with all the Hershey's Kisses you deserve Hugs and Kisses as you have begun the journey of childhood with and not against your child.

1.	Favorite color	_____
2.	Lucky number	_____
3.	Favorite season	_____
4.	Favorite time of day	_____
5.	Favorite holiday	_____
6.	Favorite hobby	_____
7.	Favorite sports activity	_____
8.	Favorite type of jewelry	_____
9.	Silver, gold or platinum	_____
10.	Preferred style of dress	_____
11.	Favorite part of body	_____

12.	Favorite outfit	_____
13.	Lucky charm	_____
14.	Favorite food	_____
15.	Favorite vegetable	_____
16.	Favorite fruit	_____
17.	Favorite cookie	_____
18.	Favorite ice cream	_____
19.	Favorite chocolate	_____
20.	Favorite candy	_____
21.	Favorite snack food	_____
22.	Favorite soft drink	_____
23.	Favorite fast food joint	_____
24.	Favorite restaurant (cheap)	_____
25.	Favorite restaurant (expensive)	_____
26.	Favorite meal	_____
27.	Favorite website	_____
28.	Favorite TV show (current)	_____
29.	Favorite TV show (old)	_____
30.	Favorite reality show	_____
31.	Favorite game show	_____
32.	Favorite TV channel	_____
33.	Favorite movie of all time	_____
34.	Favorite	_____

	adventure movie	
35.	Favorite action movie	_____
36.	Favorite animated movie	_____
37.	Favorite comedy movie	_____
38.	Favorite Broadway play	_____
39.	Favorite musical	_____
40.	Favorite actor (living)	_____
41.	Favorite actor (of any era)	_____
42.	Favorite actress(living)	_____
43.	Favorite actress(of any era)	_____
44.	Favorite fictional character	_____
45.	Favorite animated character	_____
46.	Favorite comic strip	_____
47.	Favorite comic book	_____
48.	Favorite TV cartoon	_____
49.	Favorite TV cartoon character	_____
50.	Favorite type of music	_____
51.	Favorite band	_____
52.	Favorite artist	_____
53.	Favorite type of music	_____
54.	Favorite dance tune	_____

55.	Favorite romantic song	_____
56.	Favorite chillin' song	_____
57.	Favorite song	_____
58.	Favorite role model (living)	_____
59.	Favorite role model (dead)	_____
60.	Favorite role model (fictional)	_____
61.	Favorite historical personality	_____
62.	Favorite sports (to watch)	_____
63.	Favorite athlete	_____
64.	Favorite sports team	_____
65.	Favorite board game	_____
66.	Favorite card game	_____
67.	Favorite book (fiction)	_____
68.	Favorite book (nonfiction)	_____
69.	Favorite fairy tale	_____
70.	Favorite children's book	_____
71.	Favorite religious passage	_____
72.	Favorite saying	_____
73.	Favorite poem	_____
74.	Favorite way to relax	_____
75.	Favorite to get energized	_____
76.	Favorite store	_____

77.	Favorite shopping mall	_____
78.	Favorite city	_____
79.	Favorite country	_____
80.	Favorite way to spend lazy day	_____
81.	Favorite perfume/cologne	_____
82.	Best gift ever received	_____

A Collective Group of Successful Families

If you complete every exercise in this book, You will be enjoying a creative, high energy, crazy journey of your child to adulthood. There is nothing like it. To watch them grow from babies to successful productive students enrolling in postsecondary opportunities of their choices. But more importantly you have reclaimed your youth as the " guide of the side", guiding your children to success.

I hope this book lifted your spirits and caused you to lift your child's spirits. Share the love. Share K.I.S.S. Begins At Home with friends, fellow parents and teachers.

Everyone who has children is being driven crazy equally. Turn the reading of this book into a group social activity. Schedule a discussion club/ support group. Make a topic at your parent meeting. Add food and fun. Complete the K.I.S.S. Begins At Home Homework Journal assignments together.

Share Your Stories

Did completing the assignments in this book cause you to reflect on some interesting stories? Did you have fun enjoying your child (ren)? If so, please provide us with your stories. Please send them by electronic mail to:

info@upheavalmedia.net

Or to   Ida Byrd-Hill
Upheaval Media, LLC
P.O. Box 241488
Detroit, MI 48224

Please note stories, pictures etc. will not be returned unless noted and sent with a self-addressed stamped envelope.

Index

#

1000 Places to See in the USA and Canada Before You Die — 88

A

abundance	24, 31, 32, 111
action	5, 7, 30, 47, 55, 72, 78, 98, 143, 151
adventure	86, 87, 88, 91, 97, 145, 146, 151
affection	13, 17, 18, 77, 103
American Dream	40, 41
Antoine de Saint – Exypery	56, 127
anxiety	41
Arrogance	47
Ars Amatoria	55, 126

B

Baldwin	43, 118
Beard	89, 147
Bedtime	53
Behavior	9, 93
belief	30, 32, 78
Bible	13, 34, 113
broke	23, 107
Buck	75, 138

C

capitalism	43
Chaos	13, 57
Children	28, 37, 43, 44, 54, 59, 60, 75, 80, 86, 90, 118, 138
Churchill	37, 116
circumstances	13, 31, 78, 84, 120
Cleanliness	60, 130
Compuware	7
Control and Self Control	36, 113
Courage	47
Cowardice	47
Cry the Beloved Country	15, 101

D

Death of a Showman	23, 107
Debt	41
Deceitful	47
decision	4, 34, 72
depression	18, 41, 57, 85
Detroit Public Schools	4, 44, 77
Disraeli	30, 60, 111, 130
dreams	13, 115
Duke Ellington Conservatory of Music and Art	5

E

EDP	72, 136
Education	3, 53, 62, 65, 67, 72, 73, 125, 131, 132, 133

Educational Development Plans	72
Emerson	65, 132
Enthusiasm	84
Excellence	75
Excessiveness	47

F

Failure	37, 58
field trip	33, 86, 88, 90
first teacher	8
Franklin	81, 141
Fromm	13, 96
Fuller	80, 140

G

Gide	87, 146
Global Journeys of Metro Detroit	88
Goal	56, 127, 129
goals	See goals
grades	13, 30, 53, 68, 73
Greg Godek	17

H

habits	24, 37, 53, 55, 125, 126
Hanstein Elementary	5
Hemingway	44, 121
Heraclitus	47, 122
Holiday	28, 110
home	8, 10, 21, 40, 51, 53, 54, 55, 60, 67

	68, 76, 87, 89, 94
	106, 119, 145
homes	See home
Homework	3, 11, 53, 67, 70
	89, 92, 133, 134, 155
Honesty	47
Horace	51, 124
Hugo	26, 57, 129
Hugs	18, 149
Humility	47
Hustle & TECHknow Preparatory High School	
	4, 13, 14, 15, 17
	18, 19, 22, 25, 28
	31, 33, 49, 51, 55
	56, 57, 58, 75, 77
	81, 82, 86, 90, 91

I

Impatience	47
Industrious	47
Intricate	47

J

Jackson	67, 133
Journaling	93
Jung	40, 117
Justice	47, 67, 133
juvenile delinquent	7, 44

K

King Edward	49, 123

L

La Bruyere	26, 108
Lady Sings the Blues	28, 110
laugh	52, 85, 114, 143
Lencios	84, 142
lessons	6, 8, 63, 90
lifestyle	26, 41, 43, 58, 120
Listen	45, 101, 121, 124
love	4, 13, 14, 15, 19
	26, 30, 35, 37, 58
	59, 64, 68, 87, 96
	101, 114, 120, 130
	155
Love the answer to the problem of human existence.	
	13, 96

M

Math	5, 34, 133, 134
Menander	45, 121
Mencken	21, 106
Millennials	6, 70
Millionaires	26, 27
Money	81, 109, 141
Muhammad	19, 105

N

Nash	69, 135

negative	23, 24, 25, 30, 34
	36, 41, 84, 107, 115
	126, 132
negativity	13, 25, 45
Newsweek	23, 107
Nietzsche	72, 136

O

Obscurity	47
Of Gifts of Fortune	26, 108
On Living in Baltimore	21, 106
opportunities	4, 9, 23, 24, 30
	77, 84, 155
organize	55, 60, 81, 91, 130
Ovid	55, 126

P

Parent	5, 35
passion	30, 58, 59, 115, 120
Patience	47
Paton	15, 101
patterns	37, 55
performance	4, 8, 9, 13, 36, 44
	58, 72, 75, 77, 89
	93, 135
Peter Karmanos	7
Picasso	32, 112
Plans	78
poor	13, 23, 24, 26, 28
	31, 43, 107, 108, 110
positive	23, 24, 33, 36, 84

	86, 107, 114, 126, 132
	142
Prosperity	32
Proverbs	34, 113

Q

Quran	19, 105

R

Reading	5, 7
real	27, 32, 45, 58, 65
	67, 68, 86, 112
Reap	47, 48
rules	9, 10, 15, 34, 35
	51, 53, 63, 93, 94
	125
Russell	17, 53, 103, 125

S

scarcity	23, 30, 31, 32, 111
school	4, 5, 6, 7, 8, 9
	13, 15, 16, 18, 19
	22, 28, 30, 31, 35
	40, 44, 49, 51, 53
	59, 67, 68, 71, 72
	73, 75, 76, 77, 79
	81, 85, 86, 89, 93
	94, 130, 135, 136
self-esteem	10, 18, 36, 43, 94
	113, 115

Show Kindness to your Parents.	19, 105
Simplicity	47
smile	15, 40, 101
Smiles	See smile
Sow	47, 48
Stephen Covey	44
stress	41, 57, 131
success	8, 37, 41, 47, 53, 58, 71, 72, 78, 89, 115, 155
Suspicion	47

T

Temperance	47
The Art of Loving	13, 96
The Conquest of Happiness	17, 103
The Millionaire Next Door	27
Thomas S. Szasz	36, 113
Thoreau	58, 130
thoughts	24, 25, 30, 31, 32, 93, 111
Time	81, 82, 141
Todd	23, 107
trouble	11, 16, 44, 57, 58, 80, 95

U

Uplift, Inc.	4, 90

V

values	8, 10, 28, 45, 47,

	48, 49, 76, 94, 122
violence	18, 42
Virtual education	69, 70
Vivian Grey	30, 111

W

Wisdom	63, 131
Work	3, 74, 77, 78, 138

www.ingramcontent.com/pod-product-compliance
Lightning Source LLC
Chambersburg PA
CBHW070642300426
44111CB00013B/2218